When Once Is Not Enough

Help for Obsessive-Compulsives

Gail Steketee, Ph.D.
Kerrin White, M.D.

NEW HARBINGER PUBLICATIONS, INC.

Publisher's Note

This publication is designed to provide accurate and authoritative information in regard to the subject matter covered. It is sold with the understanding that the publisher is not engaged in rendering psychological, financial, legal, or other professional services. If expert assistance or counseling is needed, the services of a competent professional should be sought.

Edited by Nina Sonenberg

First Printing September, 1990 10,000 copies

To all our patients

Contents

Foreword

In the course of treating people with Obsessive Compulsive Disorder (OCD) and their family members, we have often been asked to recommend some reading on the disorder and treatments for it. Unfortunately, all that we have had available until now is our own and others' technical writings about OCD. This book is intended to fill this gap in language we hope is clear and readily understandable to most people, regardless of prior training.

As you will see in reading case examples distributed throughout the chapters, the ideas for this book have come directly from our patients. As therapists, we have each seen hundreds of individuals with OCD. We are continually impressed with the diversity of symptoms and personalities in the people who come to us seeking treatment for this disorder. It is this diversity that makes OCD both fascinating and difficult to describe. This diversity also makes it difficult to explain treatment methods so they are applicable to all people with OCD.

This book was written with the help of many we'd like to acknowledge. First, of course, are the many patients with OCD who came to us before and during the writing of this book. It is they who led us to form many of the concepts we put forward here. The book was actually written as a series of chapters handed out at sessions of a psychoeducational group meeting of people with OCD and their family and friends. In the course of conducting this educational series, we modified chapters according to questions and feedback from members of this group. We certainly owe the group our thanks for motivating us to complete chapters in a timely manner to provide reading material to back up each lecture and discussion. We would particularly like to thank four of our patients whose names we cannot use here. A.C., A.P., J.H., and P.R. read the manuscript carefully and gave us their editorial comments and requests-to-clarify for the benefit of future readers. We believe the book is clearer and achieves its goals better for their efforts.

We also want to acknowledge the assistance of members of the staff of our OCD program, whom we do feel at liberty to name: Mary Castellana and Whitney Wykoff, who did the word processing; Sara Quay, who made editorial comments on the chapters and also helped lead the discussion groups; Steve Willis, who led discussion groups; Lee Tynes, whose excellent review on the diagnosis of OCD provided the substance of Chapter 2; and Michelle Saidel, whose review on the biological bases of OCD provided much of the substance of Chapter 3.

Gail Steketee

Kerrin White

1

Introduction and a
First-Hand Account

Mental health professionals and the public have become increasingly aware of the problem of Obsessive Compulsive Disorder (OCD). Up to two million Americans suffer from OCD right now, and as many as four million have suffered from it at some time in their lives. OCD is one of the four or five most common of all mental illnesses. Only in the past decade have mental health practitioners come to realize this.

This book is written for the patients who have OCD, for their families and friends, and for the many silent sufferers whose lives are disrupted and sometimes devastated by this disorder. The chapters in this book are designed to provide enough information about OCD to help patients and those around them understand the disorder, and make progress toward recovery. This book is also designed to help practitioners of behavior therapy for OCD.

In brief, OCD is an illness of repetitive thoughts, ideas, or images ("obsessions") which cause fear or other bad feelings such as guilt. These negative feelings in turn lead to "compulsive" or ritualistic acts or thoughts which help relieve the discomfort. OCD is defined and described in more detail in Chapter 2.

The nature and symptoms of this disorder and some hypotheses about how and why it develops are discussed in Chapters 2 through 4. Chapter 5 presents some of the research findings about psychological treatments for OCD—psychotherapy and behavior therapy—in the hope that this will guide you in selecting the best treatment strategy. It will be clear that we favor specific behavioral treatments, including exposure to feared obsessive situations and prevention of rituals, over the use of psychotherapy or "talk therapy," at least for the specific symptoms of OCD. We believe our position is well based in scientific research.

Chapters 6 through 9 give direct, practical instructions for carrying out behavioral exposure and ritual prevention by yourself or with the help of a therapist.

Medications, which we also consider useful, are discussed in detail in Chapter 10. The chapter reviews both research findings and practical considerations about use of medications alone or together with behavioral treatments. Chapter 11 details other treatments that have been used for OCD. Finally, Chapters 12 and 13 focus on preventing relapse and looking toward the future.

The emphasis throughout the book is on the *practical* application of behavior therapy and of medication treatment for people with OCD. This takes into account the possibility of a wide range of symptoms and related problems, such as depression.

For mental health practitioners who read this book, Appendix A offers specific suggestions and readings. Effective behavioral methods of treatment for most OCD sufferers require a departure from the usual once-weekly 50-minute sessions in the office. To maintain motivation and courage, more frequent and lengthy face-to-face contacts are often needed, along with availability to patients and family members by telephone when the going gets rough. A home visit by the therapist or a visit of therapist and patient to one or more exposure sites early in treatment is invaluable in understanding first hand how the OCD sufferer thinks and feels in everyday life. Such visits foster empathy and prevent treatment mistakes that can be costly. They may be less convenient for the therapist than the usual office visit, but they need not be "intrusions" into the patient's life or "violations" of treatment role boundaries.

Finally, Appendix B presents a condensed, categorized listing of obsessive-compulsive symptoms. This list is brief and general, but it can help you identify your own symptoms and see how they might be related to each other.

To begin, consider the following narrative description of OCD symptoms written by an OCD sufferer and her husband. Together, they eloquently describe the emotional struggle that this disorder can cause for both the afflicted and the family.

Help! Let Me Out!

"Why does it take you so long to do such simple things?" "If you're so aware of what you're doing, why can't you just stop?" These are questions people throw at me every week, and I don't have an answer for them. Why *can't* I stop? Why is my mind so full of fear and doubt from morning until evening, every day?

I fully realize the irrationality of my behavior. But the fear I have in my mind is so real that I must perform certain rituals every day to protect my family and myself from any wrongdoings. I guess I must believe these rituals help, or I wouldn't still be doing them. I hope that by my writing actual events that go on in my daily routine, people will begin to understand how difficult it is not only to do daily chores, but even to live each day.

I am an obsessive-compulsive disorder patient like millions of other people. I've suffered with this disorder for the past twenty years, and it has steadily grown worse with time. Some of the things in here are going to seem ridiculous and you will probably laugh, but that's OK. I laugh at them too, when I'm not doing them. It's time now to begin your journey into my mind: have fun!

Should I get up? It's 6:15. No, I better wait till 6:16, it's an even number. OK, 6:16, now I better get up, before it turns to 6:17, then I'd have to wait till 6:22.

OK, I'll get up, OK, I'm up, WAIT! I better do that again. One foot back in bed, one foot on the floor, now the other foot in bed and the opposite on the floor. OK. Let's take a shower, WAIT! That shoe on the floor is pointing in the wrong direction, better fix it. Oops, there's a piece of lint there, I better not set the shoe on top of it. Darn! There's another one over here, I can't put the shoe on top of them, I shouldn't put it between them, maybe if I move this lint over to the right, the shoe can fit in here. OH, JUST TOUCH THE SHOE TWICE AND GET OUTTA HERE!

All right, I got to the bedroom door without touching anything else, but I better step through and out again, just to be sure nothing bad will happen. THERE, THAT WAS EASY! Now to the bathroom. I better turn that light on, NO, off, NO, on, NO, off, NO, on, KNOCK IT OFF! All right, I'm done using the toilet, better flush it. OK, now spin around, wait for the toilet to finish a flush, now touch the handle, now touch the seat, remember you have to look at every screw on the toilet seat before you turn around again. OK, now turn around and touch the seat again, look at all the screws again. OK, now close the cover.

OK, let's pick out some clothes in the bedroom. First I have to get out of the bathroom. Step in, step out, step in, step out, now look at all the hinges on the bathroom door. Do this on each step, both in and out of the bathroom. OK, I'm out of the bathroom. I wonder what time it is. NO! YOU CAN'T LOOK TILL YOU ARE DONE WITH YOUR SHOWER, IF YOU LOOK BEFORE, YOU WILL BE PUNISHED.

OK, let's get some underwear. I want to wear the green ones because they fit the best, but they're lying on top of the T-shirt my grandmother gave me, and her husband (my grandfather) died last year, so I better wash those again before I wear them. If I wear them, something bad might happen. I'll wear the pink ones, even though they are all stretched out and don't stay up. They're OK because they're lying on top of an orange towel. All right, but now I need a towel. I'm allowed to use this one with the green stripe. Good.

Now let's go to the bathroom. WHOOPS! I saw the reflection of my feet when I walked by the stove, better walk back so I can see them twice. Now to the bathroom. Put one foot in the bathroom, one foot in the hall. I wonder if it would be easier to use both feet at the same time and jump in and out of the bathroom. HMMMM! I WONDER? WOULD THAT WORK? YEAH, I GUESS SO, LET'S TRY IT! It's more work, but it saves time. OK, now put the towel on the floor so it's ready when I get out of the shower. NO! I CAN'T PUT IT THERE! THERE'S A BROWN SPOT ON THE FLOOR! If I put it on top of it, something bad might happen. OK, I'll put it over here. I'll put the underwear next to the towel, but not touching the towel, and not near the brown spot. PERFECT!

OK, now let's turn the water on. Should I put the cold water on first or the hot water on first? ALWAYS A BIG DECISION! Maybe I'll put them on at the same time, with both hands touching each of them. OK, now into the tub. One foot in, now step back out, now the other foot in, now out, now in, now out, NOW IN! OK, I'm in. Now wet my hair, pick up the shampoo, put it down, pick it up, now take the cap off, put it back on, take it off again, wash hair, rinse hair, now pick up soap, put it back down again, pick it up, soap body, now put soap down. Should I put it at the front of the tub or at the back of the tub? Well, I picked it up at the front so I better put it back there. Now touch it twice with both hands. NO, TWICE DIDN'T FEEL RIGHT, START OVER, ONE, TWO, THREE, FOUR, FIVE, SIX, SEVENEIGHTNINE. Repeat once more and shut water off twice, using both hands. Step out of tub, step into tub, out, in, out, in. Now pick up towel, put back down, pick up again, dry off, now pick up underwear twice. BUT I CAN'T PUT THOSE ON IN THE BATHROOM, THAT MUST BE DONE IN THE BEDROOM, OR SOMETHING BAD MIGHT HAPPEN!

Now in and out of bathroom doorway twice, checking hinges along the way, repeat same steps into the bedroom. Now step right leg into underwear, step back out, check ALL seams on underwear and ALL tags twice, now step back in and pull on. Now let's attempt to pick out some clothes, first. Which leotard should I wear? I was thinking about wearing the orange one, so I better wear that one. OK, before I put it on I better check all seams and tags twice. Good! Now for my shorts. The gray ones are OK. Now let's put them on. Put right leg in shorts, take it back out, now put it back in, now pull up. Now pick out a shirt. Should I wear the black shirt? NO! My girlfriend said she likes shirts like that, and her father-in-law died last year, so I better wear something else. I'll wash the black one before I wear it again. I guess I'll wear the red one. YAY! That one's OK. Now first I must check all seams and tags before I put it on. OK, GOOD! OH BOY!

Now for socks. I guess I'll wear the blue ones. They're right up front, but there are the striped ones too and they match my outfit, but I already picked the blue ones first and they will feel bad if I change my mind, so I better stick with them. OK, now to put the socks on, right foot first. I have to put the sock on, now take it off, now put it back on again, check the seams on both sides of the heels, then put my foot into my shoe and then take it out and then put it back in. Now for the left foot, put the left sock halfway on, take it off and put it back on, then put the left foot halfway into the left shoe and take it back out. Oops! I forgot to check both sides of my heels before I put my foot in my shoe. START OVER! All done. Now let's tie the shoes once, untie, and redo. OK! I'M DRESSED!!!!

Now I have to dry my hair! Step in and out of the bedroom and in and out of the bathroom, check all hinges and screws on the way. OK, let's pick up the hair dryer, curling iron, brush, and hair pic all at once. Now return them to their original spots. Let's do it all over, hair dryer, curling iron, brush, and hair pic all at once. Put all items into sink, plug in hair dryer and curling iron, make sure hair dryer is plugged into top outlet, curling iron on the bottom. Now plug them in at the same time, unplug them, plug them in, unplug them, plug them in. OK! KNOCK IT OFF! OK, turn on curling iron, on, off, on, off, on, off. OK, that was six, maybe I should do nine, I can't do eight, although I don't remember why not! Nine's good, but it's not even. OH! JUST GO WITH SIX! All right, now let's turn on the hair dryer, on, off, on, off. Better stop this one now, the switch is getting loose! Let's just turn it on! — BUZZZZZZZZZZZZ It's too bad I have to dry my hair every day, it gives me too much time to just stand and think, I usually think bad things when I think too much!

Hmmmmmmm, I wonder why I do all these strange things, like touching things twice, or thinking bad thoughts? I'm sure nobody else could ever be doing the things I do. I've never seen anyone else do them. I wonder if anyone else even exists, maybe they're just there for my benefit, maybe they really are just there as characters in a play that I'm the star of. I DON'T KNOW! I can't feel what they feel, even when they communicate with me. But are they really there? I DON'T KNOW! STOP THINKING! You'll drive yourself crazy!

BUZZZZZZZZZZ——Boy it's hot in here, I better turn off the hair dryer, my hair is dry enough anyway. BUZZZZ off, on, off, on, off. OK, STOP BEFORE YOU WAKE EVERY-BODY UP! Now let's use the curling iron. Should I start curling the left side of my hair, or the right side? I guess the left side, I thought of it first. First put the hair in the curling iron, curl a few seconds, now pick up the same piece of hair and curl it again, OUCH! I burned my head with the curling iron. You better do it again. NO STUPID! That will hurt. But if I don't do it, something bad might happen to someone. SHOULD I? UGH! JUST DO IT QUICK AND GET IT DONE. OK. Ready, OUCH! OK, all set now! Let's finish my hair now, curling each piece twice.

Now it's time to spray my hair with hair spray. Let's take out the four bottles of hair spray, even though three of them are empty. OK, take the cap off of the pink bottle. This one is empty, but if I throw it away, something bad might happen to someone, so I'll spray it on my hair anyway. I have two more bottles here that are also empty. I'll spray them on my hair, too, because they'll feel left out if I don't use them. I can't play favorites. Now I'll spray the full one on my hair and I'll use the brush to comb the hair spray through my hair, then I'll use the hair pic to comb it through again. This piece of hair looks like it could use a little bit more curling. NO! YOU ARE NOT PERMITTED TO GO BACK AND USE THE CURLING IRON AGAIN, ONCE YOU HAVE SPRAYED IT AND COMBED IT, THOSE ARE THE RULES! OK, I'm all done with them. Let's unplug the hair dryer and curling iron. WAIT! You forgot to turn the curling iron off, on, off, on, off, on, off.

OK, now pull both plugs out of the outlet and put them back in, pull out, put back in, out, in, out, in, out, in, out. THOUGHTS ENOUGH! All right, pick up curling iron and hair dryer, together. Make sure to look at all seams, where appliances have been screwed together. It's been a pretty good day so far, I guess I'll try doing this only two times. Done. Hey, thoughts OK! Now let's put the appliances on the shelf. Be sure that the curling iron is nearest to the wall and the hair dryer is on the outside. Now be sure both plugs are against the wall and be sure that the "DO NOT IMMERSE IN WATER" tag is between both cords. Now pick up brush and hair pic and put them on top of the two cords. Make sure the silver tag is facing up on the brush and the brand name is facing up on the hair pic.

OK, now let's pick up each hair spray bottle separately and touch it on the shelf and back on the sink, shelf, sink, shelf, sink, shelf, one, two, three, fourfivesix. THOUGHTS ENOUGH! Now touch both hands on hair dryer, curling iron, brush, pic, and all hair sprays. Try to avoid knocking anything down or else that will become a ritual in itself. Now don't forget to touch all other bottles and tubes that are sitting on top of the cluttered shelf. Now I'm done! WAIT! I have to pick up my dirty laundry. Pick it up, now put it down. Stand up all the way straight and then bend down to pick it up again. WAIT! You didn't stand up straight enough last time. You better do it again. NO! ONCE IS ENOUGH! But I better go and do it. It's a lot easier than standing here arguing with myself about it. OK, this is straight enough. Is it straight enough? I guess so, now pick up your laundry! OK, now let's go to the laundry room. Step in and out of bathroom, twice is enough. Hey, this is a good day!

WAIT! Was that a frightening story I heard mentioned on the news? What did he go and turn that on for? I CAN'T move until the story is completed on the television. OH GREAT! THERE GOES MY GOOD DAY! Something bad happened to someone mentioned on the news. Now I'm going to have bad days for at least the next three days. OK, the story is over, now I can continue to the laundry room. Good, I got to the laundry room, but I want to make sure that what happened to that person on the news doesn't happen to us. I better go all the way back to where the television is and walk all the way back here. OK, OH NO! I have to walk past the stove again, there's the reflection of my feet again, I've got to go back and see that again, too. All right, back to the television, put the clothes down, stand up straight, and pick them up again. I have a lot of fear on my mind now. I better do this at least nine or eleven times. I know those aren't even numbers, but they are permitted since ten and eight are not. All done, now back to the laundry room. OK, I'm all ready to go out. Now all I have to do is make breakfast and dress the kids.

Let's exit my mind for a while and discuss some of what you have read. These last few pages were only the first hour of my day. You probably noticed that I've mentioned a fear of bad things happening numerous times during the morning. I have purposely failed to specify what those fears are mainly because they can be, and usually are, something different each time. My fears ordinarily only have relevance to personal happenings in my life, so I didn't feel it necessary to describe each of them individually. During many of these rituals, tension can leave me standing with fingers spread apart stiffly, arms and legs rigid. Some rituals, however, I just carry out from the habit of doing them daily, and they have no bad thoughts or tension accompanying them. I could continue to write out the rest of my day just as I have written the first hour, but this would mean hundreds of pages of boring reading. Instead I'll just highlight some of the rituals performed during the remainder of my day. Shall we proceed?

My next big decision is what to feed the kids for breakfast. If I give them cereal, I have to take out bowls and spoons and they'll need washing afterwards. Maybe I'll boil eggs, then all I have to do is crack the shells and throw them away, the kids can eat the eggs with their hands. I'll use paper cups for their milk. YAY! GOOD IDEA!

"Susan! I can't find a clean spoon!"

Uh oh. I guess "honey" is up. He knows I have trouble doing the dishes. Why does he always yell at me? If I start doing the dishes, it will take me at least an hour to clean four or five of them. I'll have to wash them so many times that my hands will be all wrinkled, and I'll be all out of breath before I'm done. I tend to neglect washing the dishes until the food on them starts to rot and mold. I guess I understand why my husband yells at me, but I hate to be yelled at, it really bothers me. I am aware of my faults, I don't need to be reminded.

"Good morning, Mommy."

Oh good, the kids are up; they make me feel good. They really seem to need me, sometimes too much maybe, but that's OK. Diane is three and a half, and Brendan is two. I feel sometimes I put too much pressure on Diane. I have so little trust in my ability to make up my own mind that I have been insisting she decide many important decisions for me since she was old enough to talk. Sometimes I make her pick out my clothes. If I am buying something new, she has to pick the color. I even ask her sometimes if it's OK just to walk into the kitchen, or if it's OK to take off my shoes. I've noticed lately she has been asking me to make decisions for her, making me say certain phrases every day at the same time. I don't know if my daughter is afflicted with OCD, or if she is just imitating me.

After the children have eaten breakfast and are dressed, we are ready to go out. I tend to try getting out of the house either with my husband or before he can take the car on his own. I have a great fear of something bad happening to family members while they are not with me. I will not allow my husband or children to go anywhere on their own. I have even gone to work every day with my husband. Fortunately, he owns his own business, so this was possible for me. Eventually he had to go out and buy a building we could both live and work in. This made things a little easier for me. Many people believe that I don't trust my husband and therefore follow him everywhere, but trust is not my problem. When a family member has to go out alone, my rituals will increase uncontrollably as visions of terrible things happening fill my mind, from the time my family leaves until they return. My husband must attend meetings out of town frequently, and I have spent as many as eight hours waiting in the car with my children. I also have trouble sending my daughter to school, and am always looking for simple excuses not to send her. This fear has been newly acquired within the last five years, and has been making for many unbearable days.

Once I have attained control of the car, I have the burden of getting into it and getting it going. This can be a big project some days, locking and unlocking the doors, rolling up and down the power windows, putting on and off the seat belts, sometimes countlessly. Once I start driving, I do fairly well. Besides the outlining of street signs with my eyes, and an occasional bad thought, driving is one time when my OCD symptoms are well-behaved. Sometimes while driving I must do overly good deeds, like letting cars out of streets in front of me, or stopping to let people cross. These are things everyone probably should do, but things I *must* do. I tend to be overly righteous, never wanting to cheat anyone in any way. If I find money on the ground, I just leave it lying there because it doesn't belong to me. My good behavior may be one instance where OCD symptoms can be useful.

My trip in the car may take us to the grocery store. Inside I have certain rituals I must perform. I am relatively subtle about how I do them to avoid drawing attention to myself. Certain foods must have their packages read several times before I am allowed to purchase them. Some things need to be touched repetitively, certain tiles on the floor must be stepped on by myself and my family. I'll find myself having to go from one end of an aisle to the other and back again, just to make everything all right. I fear being accused of shoplifting sometime because of the way I behave and the way I am always looking around to see if people have noticed my actions.

When I return home, I usually prepare lunch. I try to keep it as simple as possible, mostly just sandwiches. The less I have to do, the easier my day will be.

On a day when all has gone well, I may be able to perform some afternoon chores. I can usually hang out clothes without too much discomfort. This is mainly because I am outside where people can see me, so I try to hide my symptoms. Folding clothes is a tiresome job. Checking all tags on every article of clothing, and picking every speck of lint off them until I feel like screaming, and sometimes do, can become an all-day project. The living room floor has become my closet. After bringing the clothes in from the line, I just dump them in the middle of the floor and dig for what I need to wear. On some days the floor is barely visible.

When evening starts to set in, the terrified creature inside me starts to run wild. All of my fears are enhanced by the dark. Repetitions increase, phrases are repeated over and over in my head, some of them out loud. I start spinning in circles and jumping around. Everything must feel perfect as darkness falls. At 8:01 every evening (never before!), my prayer rituals begin. These can take anywhere from five minutes to an hour and a half, and are very private. I dislike being disturbed by anyone after I begin. If this should happen, I must start again. These must be done exactly to perfection before I am allowed to complete them. After they have reached completion, I am ready to retire for the evening in bed with the television on. A book may be nice now and then, but I have to read each page so many times that I fail to remember what I have read. I detest having to get back up after I have gone to bed, but if by some chance my assistance is required in another room, I will most often walk from room to room with my eyes closed so as not to see anything that may be out of place. I would surely have to fix it if I saw it, and this could lead to hours of repetitious touching before I got back to bed.

AHHHHH. Into bed for a good night's sleep? WRONG! Even during the night I toss and turn from one side to the other. I am allowed to sleep in only certain directions and often have bad thoughts in the night. There is really no time during the day that I am free of OCD symptoms, except maybe when I am asleep, and therefore can't enjoy it. But I try to make the most of each day and try to accomplish new feats that were previously not possible. Someday they will hopefully find a successful treatment for my disorder, but until then I am trapped inside a mind of fear and doubt with no escape. HELP! LET ME OUT!

Help Her? Help Me!

I realize that my wife has difficulties performing her daily duties, but unfortunately living with an OCD patient is no picnic and can be just as frustrating as having the disorder yourself. The whole day is spent trying to ignore her rituals, and encouraging her to do some household chores—or anything, for that matter. She is difficult to put up with and even to *be* with sometimes.

The day usually begins an hour before I want it to. My wife is always up an hour before me and proceeds to do some sort of bouncing ritual on the bed. I try not to get up until she is out of the bathroom. If I'm running late some days, I must get in there while she is still "ritualizing." She makes going to the bathroom a chore for me. She stands in my way and spins in circles, bumping into me. Then she begins again and does the whole thing over: the touching, the moving, and the looking, and again I'm in the way. I don't dare try to shower yet.

Nobody likes doing the dishes, and my wife is no exception. She will let them pile up until all the dishes in the house are dirty. She will hide dirty dishes in boxes in the closet and wherever there is empty space. I usually resist doing them myself until I get so mad I can't stand the mess. To remedy the problem, I washed all my wife's dishes, pots, and pans, wrapped them up, and hid them from her. I left her one fork, one spoon, one knife, one of everything she needs so she must wash it before she can use it again. My intentions were noble, but the attempt was futile; I still have dirty dishes.

Finding something to wear in the laundry is a 10-minute search. To start with, she can't put clothes in the machine, so I do. If I don't, the pile gets so big it takes two days to wash it all. Our son is two years old and is potty training. He has frequent accidents. This leaves the clothes smelling bad and it is an embarrassment to have guests visit. Therefore, I put a load of laundry in the machine in the morning. My wife will hang everything out on the line and bring it all in. I think she feels guilty that people will see her doing her touching when she is outside, so she behaves herself. Unfortunately, as soon as she does bring the clothes inside, she dumps them on the living room floor. Putting them away is too much to hope for. We just dig for the day's outfit. GOOD LUCK!

Cleaning the kitchen is done about every three weeks and that is usually by me. The mess is unbelievable! I will come in from work at about 9:00 at night and will clean until about 12:00. The stove smokes when you turn it on from things spilled on the burners. The counter, too, is not just sticky, but has hard bumps of food stuck to it. I find hard, moldy bread lying around and milk that has gone beyond souring. I don't dare look in the microwave. I try to keep things up every day, but it does not stay that way long; she and the kids destroy the kitchen.

Floors are made to walk on, but not ours! The living room floor is for our laundry. The kitchen floor is so sticky that you could lose a shoe if it is not laced tightly.

When cleaning the bedroom, I actually take the bed and stand it upright against the wall. Under the bed many things can be discovered: old paper cups, food, toys, etc. I vacuum. Then I get out the sponge and a pail. The night stands are caked with "I don't know what." The whole room smells bad. I clean it and say, "Surprise, Honey!"

I could write for hours about the different things my wife does and doesn't do. You are probably wondering, "Why did you marry her?" When we first met, she used to hide her OCD symptoms. Every now and then, I would catch her doing something unusual, but it wasn't too bad; in fact, some things were cute. Now she hides when we go places; she hides in stores. Why? I don't know.

Our sex life was imaginative, creative, and fun. Now, I "contaminate" her. I don't even feel like asking her anymore.

She takes good care of the kids, surprisingly. I think she is afraid they might say something to embarrass her in front of somebody. I think the real drastic changes started when she was pregnant with our first child and was sick for nine months. I thought at the time it would pass after the baby was born, but it only got worse. We have two children now and my wife is worse than ever.

After seeing the Phil Donahue show, we realized she had OCD. Now she blames everything on OCD, like it's OK to do now. I am getting burnt out. I work for myself, which requires many hours. I can't get sufficient sleep with her bouncing on the bed and her blowing on her fingers. She wonders why I am so grumpy. We have been for medication treatment for three months, but so far nothing has helped. Somebody help her? Help me!

2

Do You Have Obsessive Compulsive Disorder?

What Is Obsessive Compulsive Disorder?

Obsessive Compulsive Disorder (OCD) is an illness. It is also a psychiatric diagnosis. One thing to realize right away is that these two things—the illness and the diagnosis—are not necessarily the same.

If this confuses you, consider the fact that the official definitions of psychiatric diagnoses have changed repeatedly over the years. Probably, the illnesses have not changed—much, at least—but mental health professionals have changed the way they look at these illnesses and define them. The hope is that the definitions of diagnoses come closer to matching the illnesses themselves as more is learned.

In the United States, psychiatric diagnosis mostly follows rules set forth in a publication of the American Psychiatric Association (APA) called the *Diagnostic and Statistical Manual of Mental Disorders* (DSM for short). Every few years, the APA revises DSM in a new edition: DSM-I, DSM-II, DSM-III. The current version is the *Diagnostic and Statistical Manual of Mental Disorders, Third Edition, Revised* (DSM-III-R). Even now, the APA is working on DSM-IV, but we will be talking about diagnosis in terms of DSM-III-R. It's the best and most widely accepted definition in the field now, but keep in mind that it is not the last word. It may *not* correctly define what OCD really is in all its possible forms. For example, DSM-III-R excludes from the diagnosis of OCD the common problem of hair-pulling (trichotillomania), which some experts believe is really just another form of OCD.

How can such differences of opinion arise? Take as an example the infectious venereal disease syphilis, which was once a much larger public health problem than it is today. In the early stages of the illness, what is called "primary syphilis" causes only a skin lesion. In its later stages, "tertiary syphilis" can cause degeneration of the brain. These two conditions—primary and tertiary syphilis—look very different on first encounter. What ties them together is that both are caused by the same syphilis bacterium, the spirochete. In both primary and tertiary syphilis, the laboratory can find antibodies to the bacterium or even see the spirochete itself under a microscope.

Unfortunately, OCD—like most psychiatric disorders—has nothing like a spirochete that can be identified clearly and reliably in a laboratory. So deciding whether two psychiatric conditions, which look somewhat similar and somewhat different at the same time, are really the same illness or not demands a lot of educated guesswork. Later, this process will be examined more closely. For now, you know enough to take these diagnostic guidelines "with a grain of salt." Still, their specific wording and meaning is followed closely. That's the only way to ensure everyone means the same thing in using a diagnostic label like "OCD."

The rules (criteria) for diagnosing OCD have actually not changed a lot from DSM-I to DSM-II to DSM-III to DSM-III-R. Essentially, the definition is simple, but read it carefully:

THE ESSENTIAL FEATURES OF OBSESSIVE COMPUL-SIVE DISORDER ARE REPEATED OBSESSIONS OR COMPULSIONS (not necessarily both) THAT ARE SIG-NIFICANTLY DISTRESSING OR TIME-CONSUMING OR THAT CAUSE SIGNIFICANT INTERFERENCE WITH SOCIAL OR OCCUPATIONAL FUNCTIONING.

Note that either obsessions *or* compulsions are enough to make a diagnosis of OCD. Most OCD sufferers have both, but some have only one or the other. Note, too, the important requirement that these symptoms be *significantly* distressing or time-consuming or interfere *significantly* with your functioning. "Normal" people may occasionally, even repeatedly, have unwanted thoughts (such as an urge to hurt someone) or behaviors (such as superstitious habits) that do not cause enough distress or impairment to warrant any treatment or diagnosis. Indeed, almost everyone may have such "symptoms" at one time or another! Usually, it's quite clear that the symptoms of the OCD sufferer are not within the "normal" range and do more than cause "significant" distress or impairment. These symptoms may make you miserable or nearly incapacitate you. They may take up hours a day. But sometimes, in milder cases, it can be hard to tell where to draw the line between the normal and the pathological. It also becomes complicated when you have another disorder besides OCD—for example, depression—that seems to be causing many of your problems. If your obsessive-compulsive symptoms seem to be only a minor piece of a much bigger picture, perhaps they do not require a separate diagnosis. You'll find more about that later in this chapter.

First you need to be clear on the meaning of the two words that both name and define OCD: obsessions and compulsions.

What Are Obsessions?

DSM-III-R defines obsessions in the following way:

> OBSESSIONS ARE PERSISTENT IDEAS, THOUGHTS, IMPULSES, OR IMAGES THAT ARE EXPERIENCED, AT LEAST INITIALLY, AS INTRUSIVE OR SENSELESS.

Note that both this definition and the definition of compulsions given later emphasize repetitive, persistent experiences—experiences that happen over and over again in a fairly consistent way. A single thought that happens once would not qualify, however upsetting it may be. In the most typical OCD sufferer, a given obsession may occur hundreds or thousands of times.

Note also the requirement that the obsession be experienced—at least at first—as intrusive or senseless. This means that you do not want the thought and would like to be rid of it. As a result, you might try to push it out of your mind, only to have it come back again and again.

In contrast, a depressed person without OCD might brood on something that seems to him or her quite important to think about, like financial troubles. This does not fit the definition of an obsession used here. If unproductive worrying of this sort takes up a lot of time and becomes a problem in itself, you might call this *rumination* instead.

A different example of a preoccupation that is not an obsession would be someone who firmly believes his food to be poisoned even though there is no real evidence to support this. You would call this a *delusion*.

Yet another example would be a person who devotes an excessive amount of time and attention to something—a project, a romantic attachment—that is neither obviously crazy nor particularly bothersome to the person himself, although it may be bothersome to other people because it is extreme. This is called *overvalued ideation*. None of these phenomena are true obsessions, although they may be related in some cases to OCD. True obsessions are generally thoughts or ideas that you can see don't make sense even though you worry about them.

There may come times in the course of OCD when you lose sight of the fact that your obsessions don't make sense, when you do start to believe in them. But much of the time, especially early in the illness, most OCD sufferers have a different perspective. Obsessions feel like *symptoms*. Sometimes these thoughts and experiences can be confused with "worries." But if the worries seem ridiculous, even to you, they are probably obsessions. For example, someone who is having trouble paying bills might worry about this excessively, to the point of rumination; but someone who has enough money and knows it, but still spends hours he doesn't want to spend imagining financial catastrophes that don't seem likely even to him, may be obsessive.

Note that obsessions don't have to be thoughts. The definition allows for obsessive *impulses* and *images*. Perhaps obsessive *feelings* should be allowed as well. Obsessions can take many forms. Among the most common obsessions are thoughts of doing harm to others—to someone you are *not* angry with and don't really wish to harm, even to someone you love. These obsessions may take the form of a *fear* that you might harm that person, or of a mental *picture* of violence. Another common obsession is a sense of *doubt* that you really did something properly—"Did I really lock the door (turn off the gas, shut off the faucet, unplug the iron, etc)?" There may be associated obsessive fears that burglars will break in, the house will burn down, and so forth. Also common is the obsessive fear that something is contaminated—with dirt, germs, broken glass, chemical toxins, etc. Sometimes there is the obsessive sense that something is just not "right"—not correctly arranged or ordered or not done in the right way or sequence. An obsession may be as simple as a single meaningless word that keeps repeating itself in your mind, or as complex as a vast array of different "worries" with complicated mental explanations behind them.

One way for people to think about obsessions (and how much of a problem they can be) is to consider the common experience of having a jingle in your head that keeps replaying itself in an annoying way. This can be an example of a "normal" obsession that doesn't last long enough or cause enough trouble to qualify for a diagnosis of OCD. In some cases though, it could represent a real symptom of OCD. The question is how much it interferes with normal functioning, and how long it lasts or how much energy it consumes. Suppose that jingle ran through your head all day, every day?

An important characteristic of most obsessions is that they cause anxiety or tension. In fact, some experts prefer to define obsessions in this way, as "anxiety-provoking mental experiences." On the other hand, it is possible that obsessions can provoke other kinds of unpleasant feelings besides anxiety—for example, guilt or disgust. It is also possible, at least according to DSM-III-R, that obsessions might merely take up time and attention, interfering with concentration, and be unwanted for this reason without causing real emotional distress. However, the *usual* anxiety-provoking nature of obsessions helps distinguish obsessions from another possible symptom of OCD—cognitive (mental) compulsions. Cognitive compulsions, in contrast to obsessions, generally *relieve* anxiety rather than raise it. They will be discussed in the next section of this chapter.

Finally, OCD sufferers can usually recognize obsessions as products of their own minds, even if unwanted. If words that plague you seem to come from outside your head, like external voices, they are more likely auditory hallucinations or illusions than obsessions. Similarly, if a distressing image is not a *mental* picture but appears in space before your eyes and seems quite real, it is more likely a visual hallucination or illusion. Usually this distinction is clear, but sometimes it can be difficult to make. Some obsessive-compulsive people may refer to their obsessive thoughts as "inner voices," which can confuse even a psychiatrist into thinking they are hallucinations!

What Are Compulsions?

DSM-III-R defines compulsions in the following way:

> COMPULSIONS ARE REPETITIVE, PURPOSEFUL, AND INTENTIONAL BEHAVIORS THAT ARE PERFORMED IN RESPONSE TO AN OBSESSION, ACCORDING TO CERTAIN RULES, OR IN A STEREOTYPED FASHION. THEY MAY BE DESIGNED TO NEUTRALIZE OR TO PREVENT DISCOMFORT OR SOME DREADED EVENT OR SITUATION.

Compulsions are often considered the hallmark of OCD, maybe because they are often observable to others in a way that obsessions are not. However, perhaps 20 percent of OCD sufferers have only obsessions without any apparent compulsions. One way of classifying types of OCD separates this group of "pure obsessionals" and categorizes the rest by their specific compulsive behaviors: washers, checkers, repeaters, and so forth.

The classic case is the handwasher. Whether or not you have this specific problem, you may find it useful to consider this as an example to better understand the meaning of obsessions and compulsions.

The handwasher usually has obsessive fears of contamination—for example, by germs (one of many possible contaminants). The washer may feel that various objects and surfaces—for example, doorknobs—are contaminated with germs, which get on his hands when he touches them. He then fears spreading these germs by his hands to other parts of his body or other objects, where they might make him or others sick. Feeling anxious about this contamination on his hands, he washes them, which generally makes him feel better, at least temporarily. However, the handwashing may not seem to him good enough unless he does it for an especially long time, or repeats it a certain number of times, or uses especially hot water, or takes care not to touch the faucet in the process. In any case, he usually finds himself recontaminated again soon after he has gotten clean, so that the handwashing process needs to be repeated many times a day. This may leave his hands red and raw. It may also take up a lot of time, causing delays in getting other things done.

Think about how this handwashing meets the definition for a compulsion. It is a behavior that is repetitive. It is purposeful—the purpose being to remove contaminants. It is intentional—the washer knows what he is doing or about to do and "intends" to do it, even though at the same time he may consider it "sick" behavior and try to fight it. It does not take him by surprise, in an involuntary way, like a tic (which will be discussed later). The washing is performed in response to the obsessive fear or feeling of contamination. It is often performed in a very specific way—for a certain length of time or with just so many rinses and washes before it is done. It is designed to neutralize the distress of feeling contaminated and to prevent the feared result of contaminating others or getting sick oneself.

As you can see, the example of compulsive handwashing fits the definition of compulsion very well. Of course, this is a classic example on which the definition is based. Another classic example is checking. A checker may repeatedly go back to check a lock, in response to the obsessive fear or doubt that she has really locked the door. Each time she checks the lock, it reassures her, at least a little, but often not for long. As she leaves the door, she wonders if she really got it right; she may have to go back and recheck it many times before she can let it be. The purpose of the behavior is to reduce the possibility of someone breaking in, and it would make sense except that it has to be repeated so many times that you know it is a waste of time. Most people might check something like this, but only once.

In contrast, other OCD sufferers who repeat certain actions may do so out of a "magical" or "superstitious" sense that, unless they do so, some disaster will happen that is not at all logically connected to their actions. For example, one woman may spend a lot of time repeating a certain phrase—until she feels she has "gotten it just right"—out of the obsessive fear that if she does not do so, her mother may die. She "knows" this makes no sense at all, just as you "know" a black cat won't bring bad luck, but she feels anxious anyway. The variety of such "repeating" or "ordering" behaviors is potentially limitless, but commonly it includes walking through doorways in a certain manner, arranging objects in specific ways, and repeating actions such as touching an object a certain number of times.

Some of this repetitive, superstitious behavior may be done mentally—for example, by counting or praying silently. This brings up the idea of "cognitive compulsions" mentioned earlier. Some people feel that thinking about something in a certain way is necessary to avert danger. These cognitive compulsions (such as making a mental list to prevent forgetting, or forming a "good" thought to counteract a "bad" one) are important to distinguish from obsessions because their treatment in behavior therapy is different. Their hallmark is that they *reduce* anxiety, rather than increase it as obsessions do.

Compulsive behaviors may take other, subtler forms. For example, one common response to obsessive fears is to seek reassurance from others. You might look to your doctor to reassure you that you don't have cancer or AIDS for instance. This reassurance, once obtained, may give temporary relief but often leads to further reassurance-seeking, which can exasperate others. It may take the form of repetitive questioning, telephoning, arguing, etc. It is important to recognize this for what it is because it may call for a very different response from therapists, friends, and family than what most people are inclined to do—that is, they should probably *not* provide the reassurance the OCD sufferer demands. There will be more on this topic in the chapter on "Stopping Rituals."

Yet another form that compulsive behavior may take is *hoarding,* often of worthless objects or even garbage. Sometimes this is motivated by the obsessive fear that the person might throw out something of eventual use or of great importance. Usually such people do *not* have such a clear understanding that their saving is senseless.

Finally, *slowness* is a common problem in OCD. This may be the result of having to do many rituals in the course of ordinary activities, or may represent a type of compulsive behavior in itself. For example, a person may become so meticulous in doing ordinary things like eating or dressing "just right" that these activities take hours and allow little time for anything else during the day.

In addition to the many different types of obsessive and compulsive behaviors that are the essential features of the *diagnosis* of OCD, OCD usually involves other symptoms that are not so necessary to the diagnosis. That is to say, these symptoms can often occur in other illnesses as well. The following section describes some of these symptoms.

Other Symptoms of OCD

DSM-III-R groups OCD together with certain other diagnoses—generalized anxiety disorder, agoraphobia, social phobia, simple phobia, panic disorder, post-traumatic stress disorder—as all belonging to the class of "anxiety disorders." This is the most common type of mental disorder in the general population. Other *classes* of disorders include affective disorders (for example, depression and mania), impulse control disorders (for example, trichotillomania), organic mental disorders (for example, Alzheimer's disease), and substance abuse disorders (for example, alcoholism).

It is still not completely clear whether OCD "belongs" more with the anxiety disorders than with another class, such as affective disorders or impulse control disorders. However, anxiety—the feeling of fear in the absence of any logical danger—is very common in OCD. Also, anxiety plays a key role in behavioral theory as to how obsessive-compulsive symptoms come about, as you will see in a later chapter.

When the anxiety seems clearly related to the obsessions, as when the washer becomes nervous after touching a doorknob, it is considered part of the OCD. But if anxiety, especially when associated with *physical* symptoms of tension (such as racing heartbeat, shortness of breath, etc.), occurs in other situations or unpredictably, it may mean the presence of still another anxiety disorder, such as Panic Disorder or Generalized Anxiety Disorder, in addition to the OCD.

Another common characteristic of OCD that links it to the other anxiety disorders is *avoidance* behavior. Avoidance is especially typical of phobic patients. Compulsive washers have sometimes been described as "germ phobics." One difference is that the obsessive-compulsive patient, even the washer, often cannot avoid what he fears as completely as, say, a phobic patient may avoid heights. But sometimes the obsessive-compulsive patient succeeds in avoiding contamination so thoroughly that there is little need for compulsive washing. In such cases, the avoidance behavior itself is often the biggest problem. The person may simply isolate himself in his house, or in his room, and greatly limit his contacts with the outside world. The famous case of Howard Hughes was one example of this; at the end of his life he lived like a hermit, avoiding germs by secluding himself.

Depression is also very common in OCD. In contrast to OCD itself, which tends to persist in varying degrees for years and years in most sufferers, depression tends to come and go in "episodes." When a depressive episode is severe enough to disrupt functioning—to affect sleeping, eating, energy, concentration—it may deserve an additional diagnosis, such as Major Depression.

At one time, in an earlier edition of DSM, such a diagnosis as Major Depression would have excluded the diagnosis of OCD, which would have been considered "secondary" to the depression. The same "exclusionary" principle would have applied to other "primary" diagnoses, such as Schizophrenia, Bipolar Disorder (manic-depressive illness), or Tourette's Syndrome (characterized by tics). Now the diagnostic practice is different: when you meet the criteria for more than one disorder, you get more than one diagnosis. This new practice may be helping to increase the frequency with which people are diagnosed as having OCD; no longer do other diagnoses get "priority."

Nevertheless, there are still some disorders that may take the place of OCD in diagnostic terms. Some of these disorders may really be different types of OCD, but DSM-III-R calls them by different names (see below). Others may be distinct illnesses in themselves, but in some way also close "relatives" of OCD. This is one area where the diagnostic system may change as more is learned about how these different illnesses relate to each other.

Do You Have Something "Like" OCD?

"Compulsive" hair-pulling (trichotillomania) is one common example of such a condition. Some people pull out their hair, usually from the head, because it eases tension. Nevertheless, they also make efforts to stop themselves, even tying up their own hands at night! Hair-pulling may result in unsightly bald spots that require a wig. This is a lot like OCD in many ways, except that there is rarely an obsession behind the compulsive pulling of hair, unless it is the urge to pull itself. Also, hair-pullers sometimes report that it "feels good," unlike compulsive washing or checking. Others just find themselves unconsciously doing it, like a habit. For such reasons, trichotillomania is classified with "impulse control disorders." These include also nail-biting and compulsive stealing (kleptomania). Kleptomania may also closely re-semble OCD, particularly when the object stolen is of no value or use to the kleptomaniac, who may simply throw it away. But again, there is often no obsessive thought behind the stealing, which sometimes causes pleasure as well as release of tension.

Hypochondriacs often seem "obsessed" with physical illnesses. If a hypochondriac is absolutely *convinced* he has an illness despite contrary evidence from laboratory tests and doctors, he is not obsessive but *delusional*. However, many hypochondriacs are not *sure* they have a certain illness, but worry that they *might*. These people find the doctors' reas-surances at least temporarily a relief. If the hypochondriac keeps going to doctor after doctor in search of more and more reassurance, this begins to look a lot like the compulsive reassurance-seeking common to OCD.

Yet another type of person is preoccupied with an imag-ined or exaggerated defect in his or her physical body. This is sometimes called "dysmorphophobia" or body dysmor-phic disorder. For example, such a person may be concerned that his nose is too large, even though it looks all right to most observers, and may seek plastic surgery to correct it.

Another type of person who may become "obsessed" with imagined defects in physical appearance is the person with an eating disorder, such as Anorexia Nervosa or Bulimia (binge-eating). Such people often feel themselves to be fat, even when thin or of normal weight for their height. Or they may have *fears* of getting fat. Often they have rituals around eating. Eating, especially binge-eating, may cause great anxiety, which is relieved by purging—for example, causing oneself to throw up. The fears of being overweight and the purging have characteristics of obsessive and of compulsive behavior: the former increase anxiety and the latter relieve it. The binge-eating also may have "compulsive" characteristics, with surprisingly little pleasure involved; some bulimic patients binge on such unappetizing objects as melon rinds or bread flour.

All of these disorders—trichotillomania, kleptomania, hypochondriasis, body dysmorphic disorder, anorexia, bulimia—have certain obsessive-compulsive characteristics but are currently given different diagnostic labels. If you have such a disorder, you may also receive a diagnosis of OCD, but only if you have other symptoms of an obsessive-compulsive nature that fall *outside* the first diagnosis. For example, if you are an anorexic with cleaning rituals, you may have both Anorexia Nervosa and OCD; but if all your rituals have to do with food, you do not qualify for a diagnosis of OCD, just anorexia. The fact that such combinations of illnesses occur quite commonly in the same people adds to the suspicion that they may be related.

Still other illnesses may bear a similar relationship to OCD. Morbid jealousy and infatuation (as in the well-known movie *Fatal Attraction*) and some sexual disorders, such as exhibitionism, are examples.

A case that deserves special consideration is Gilles de la Tourette's Syndrome, often called simply "Tourette's Syndrome." This illness is characterized by tics. Tics are repetitive behaviors distinguished from compulsions by the lack of a sense of purpose or intention; they come on "involuntarily." They are often simple movements, such as squinting of the eye, but may be quite complicated, such as spoken words. Sometimes in practice it is difficult to tell whether a given behavior is better called a tic or a compulsion. But often a patient with tics from Tourette's Syndrome may also have clear obsessive-compulsive symptoms as well. Furthermore, relatives of Tourette's patients have an increased risk of having either Tourette's themselves—or OCD. This suggests a special relationship between Tourette's Syndrome and OCD, which has yet to be understood.

Be careful to keep in mind that not all repetitive behaviors are "compulsive" in the sense of OCD. In OCD, rituals are usually driven by anxiety, not pleasure or gain, and the ritualizer has a sense that the ritual is irrational and makes efforts to fight it. Autistic people (such as in the movie *Rain Man*) may have rituals without any sense of their being senseless, or any impulse to fight them. This may also happen with psychotic individuals. Such behaviors are sometimes called "stereotypic," not compulsive. Alcoholics, drug abusers, gamblers, and many sexual deviants may refer to their behavior as "compulsive" and even fight it, but they also get a lot of pleasure out of it. This element of pleasure is not present for obsessive-compulsives.

Does Having OCD Mean You Have an Obsessive-Compulsive Personality?

The answer to this question—contrary to what used to be thought—is *probably not*. The obsessive-compulsive personality is defined in DSM-III-R in a way quite different from OCD. Personality disorders in general are thought of as representing a lifelong set of traits or characteristic patterns of behavior. The individual experiences these traits as part of himself, not as an illness that afflicts him. He (or she) may recognize these traits as causing trouble at times, but not as unwanted intrusive symptoms.

Different types of personality disorders include the antisocial type (often thought of as the criminal type), the histrionic (hysterical) type, and so forth. The obsessive-compulsive personality disorder is said to be marked by a "pervasive pattern of perfectionism and inflexibility" with at least five out of nine characteristics: perfectionism; preoccupation with details; insistence that others submit to one's way of doing things; excessive devotion to work; indecisiveness; overconscientiousness; restricted ability to express emotion; lack of generosity; or inability to discard worthless objects.

In fact, only a minority of OCD sufferers actually fit the above description for obsessive-compulsive personality disorder. It is clear that people with very different personality types may have OCD. On the other hand, there may be *some* relationship between obsessive-compulsive personality disorder as described above and OCD. For example, the person with obsessive slowness may be quite perfectionistic about doing ordinary things, like brushing his or her teeth. An inability to discard worthless objects is very similar to compulsive hoarding. The key difference seems to be that the OCD sufferer realizes this behavior doesn't make sense and fights it (although sometimes the OCD patient may lose this "insight" or stop fighting), whereas the obsessive-compulsive personality accepts and even defends his or her compulsive actions. It is common for us to hear from our OCD patients that one of their parents seemed to do things compulsively without being bothered by this behavior, as far as our patient could tell. Perhaps the parent had obsessive-compulsive personality traits, suggesting that these do have *some* relationship to OCD.

The relationship between OCD and personality is still cloudy. Nevertheless, it is useful to keep the distinction in your mind. Not all people with OCD are workaholics; some may even be lazy! Not all are meticulously neat and clean; even compulsive cleaners may be quite messy in areas outside their obsessive concerns. And not all, by any means, are cold or miserly; many are warm, generous, likeable people. In fact, many, if not most, OCD sufferers have quite "normal" personalities.

How Common Is OCD and Whom Does It Affect?

OCD is very common indeed. In fact, it may be the fourth most common of all mental disorders—after phobias, depression, and alcoholism. It seems to affect about 2 percent of the general population—that is, two persons out of every hundred. To some people, this may not seem like a lot. In contrast to OCD, for example, almost everyone gets the common cold. But colds last an average of a week or 10 days, whereas OCD typically lasts most of a lifetime. As a result, at any given point in time there might be almost as many people with OCD as there are with colds! The currently estimated prevalence of OCD is about *50 times* what was once thought.

Why was this illness, now known to be quite common, once thought to be so rare? In general, OCD sufferers are embarrassed by, even ashamed of, their symptoms. They often feel they suffer from a lack of self-control, a failure of reason, or a "craziness" that sets them apart from others. As a result, they often try to hide their problems. Because they are not really crazy, and are rarely violent or destructive, they may succeed in hiding their problems much better than psychotic people who have lost contact with reality completely or depressed people who have become suicidal. It is not unusual for the closest relative of the OCD patient to be relatively unaware of what the person has been suffering. It is not even unusual for a therapist whom the patient has been talking to for years to be unaware!

Another reason OCD sufferers have not "come out of the closet" until recently is that they had little reason to hope for help. Once thought rare, OCD received little publicity or research attention until the past several years. It was considered very difficult to treat and not very responsive to treatment at a time when the most common treatment was psychotherapy. Only recently has it become widely known that both behavior therapy and medications can be of great help.

Despite OCD having been so long a "secret" illness, it is clear that this affliction goes back a long time in history. Famous sufferers include John Bunyan, who wrote the early English novel *The Pilgrim's Progress;* the English writer Samuel Johnson; and the religious reformer Martin Luther.

It is also clear that OCD affects people of all ages and both sexes. It usually begins early in life—in childhood, adolescence, or young adulthood—and often continues into old age. In childhood, males are more often affected, but later in life the sex ratio is more nearly equal. OCD most commonly follows a chronic course with waxing and waning symptoms over the course of years, less commonly clearing up completely or progressing downhill into total incapacitation.

OCD is especially important to identify right now because there has been a surge of research interest and support for studying the illness. New aspects are being studied, such as brain metabolism. New treatments are being developed, such as novel drugs. This is an opportunity for you to contribute to the process—and get help for yourself—by helping researchers develop a better understanding of this common yet debilitating illness. Keep an open mind about participating in such research when it is available to you.

Summary

The essential features of OCD are repeated obsessions or compulsions that are distressing or cause significant interference with functioning. Obsessions are persistent ideas, thoughts, impulses, or images that are felt by the sufferer to be intrusive and senseless. These are distinguished from rumination (unproductive worrying about real problems) and from delusions (ideas held to be realistic when, in fact, there is no evidence to support them). Overvalued ideas occur when a person believes that his or her obsessive fears are founded in realistic dangers.

Compulsions are repeated behaviors or thoughts designed to relieve the discomfort provoked by obsessive thoughts. Washing, cleaning, checking, repeating actions, putting objects in order, hoarding or saving things are common behavioral compulsions. Praying rituals, mental listing, repeating or rearranging in your mind certain words or phrases are common mental rituals. Most people with OCD also avoid certain situations, places, or objects because they provoke fear or discomfort. Many people with OCD are also depressed.

Some psychological disorders like trichotillomania, hypochondriasis, body dysmorphic disorder, kleptomania, anorexia and bulimia resemble OCD quite closely, in that certain "compulsive" actions are carried out to neutralize anxiety. Currently, however, these disorders are not considered the same as OCD, though they may be related and even respond to similar treatment.

Some people have personality traits that can be called obsessive-compulsive but that do not usually have anxiety, guilt, or discomfort associated with them. These personality traits are not considered the same as OCD and are not necessary to the development of OCD, but may also be related to OCD in some respects.

3

Biological Bases of OCD

Biological versus Psychological: The Wrong Question

A lot of people—many psychiatrists and psychologists included—like to think that mental illness must be either biological *or* psychological in nature. According to them, either you have a biological illness (such as a hereditary abnormality in brain biochemistry), or you have a psychological problem (such as an emotional conflict resulting from childhood upbringing).

This book takes a different viewpoint—that Obsessive Compulsive Disorder (OCD), like a lot of other illnesses, probably results from many factors, some biological and some psychological, acting together to cause the disease. In some diseases, it may be clear that one factor predominates: for example, in the hereditary neurological disease Huntington's chorea, there is such a strong genetic factor that if you inherit the specific genetic defect, you will almost always get the disease; without it, you won't. But in most illnesses, no single factor has such complete control.

Consider an example. If atherosclerotic heart disease runs in your family, you may be born with a predisposition to a heart attack. If you also have a high cholesterol level in your blood, your blood vessels may get clogged and hasten a heart attack. If you are also overweight and have high blood pressure or smoke, this adds to the strain on your heart and further increases your risk. So far, all these seem to be straightforward biological factors in an unquestionably "biological" disease. But why do you smoke, have high cholesterol, excess weight, and high blood pressure? The reasons may be partly hereditary, but diet, exercise, and stress—"lifestyle"—all play a part. Certainly, psychological factors play a role in your lifestyle!

With so many *physical* illnesses resulting from a combination of biological and psychological factors, *mental* illnesses seem quite likely to originate in this way as well. The brain is a physical organ of the body that is engineered to react to your environment and experience.

Why make such an obvious point? Many people are tempted to simplify the complicated and confusing issues surrounding mental illness into a single cause, which would be easier to grasp. When a certain biological abnormality is found to be associated with OCD, it is tempting to point to it as evidence that OCD is the result of some one specific problem with the brain. That also makes it easier to believe that researchers are on the verge of figuring out the problem and finding a solution.

The truth is that researchers are a long way from understanding how the brain works in health, let alone in disease. The little pieces of the biological puzzle you'll find in this chapter do not even begin to prove that OCD is "simply" a biological illness.

The danger is that people who believe such a simple way of thinking about it—especially people who suffer from OCD and people who live with OCD sufferers—will cut them-selves off from any treatment save a biological one, usually a pill. The old saying, "Biological treatments for biological illnesses; psychological treatments for psychological illnes-ses," sounds good but is quite wrong. Such a simple psycho-logical treatment as relaxation training can help the clearly physical condition of high blood pressure. And doesn't the "biological" treatment of aspirin help relieve even the ten-sion headache that results from a fight with your boss?

In OCD—as in many illnesses—there are probably many biological and psychological factors that affect the develop-ment and course of the disorder. Most importantly, both biological and psychological treatments can help, and neith-er should be ignored because of a simplistic theory about the cause being of one type or the other. This is the first word of caution. One more is needed before we go on to look at what is being found out about biological abnormalities in OCD.

Facts versus Findings: Let the Buyer Beware!

The second chapter made a distinction between the *illness* OCD and the *diagnosis* OCD. The point was that how a condition is *defined* in a diagnostic system is not necessarily the truth about what the condition really *is*. This chapter will make a similar type of distinction: between *findings* and *facts*.

A finding is what one researcher reports after analyzing the results of a study he has done. It is what he presents at a meeting or writes up for a professional journal, where it sometimes gets picked up and publicized in the popular media. Most other scientists understand that what the first scientist *found* is not necessarily a *fact*; but many lay people may not.

Quite apart from the rare scientist who deliberately lies or distorts results to make for a sensational "finding," many genuine researchers simply cannot confirm one another's results. This is especially true in the field of mental health, where human studies are hard to control very well and where animal studies don't have much relevance to human ailments.

For example, if scientists want to compare functioning of one brain hormone in two different groups of rats, they can make sure that these rats are raised and kept under similar conditions—with identical diets, exposure to light, opportunities for activity, etc. They can implant electrodes or insert chemicals directly into specific areas of the rats' brains; they can sacrifice the animals and examine their brain cells microscopically. In contrast, clinical researchers with human subjects can do virtually none of this. They must accept the fact that OCD subjects and "normal" control subjects may lead very different lives, and come from very different backgrounds, even though they are "matched" on basic factors like age and sex. Any measures of the brain hormone that researchers use with human subjects must be indirect, such as hormone levels in easily available blood platelets rather than in the brain itself; these indirect measures may have little to do with the hormone's functioning in the brain. Many "uncontrolled" factors—such as different amounts of physical activity in different subjects—may produce findings of abnormalities in OCD that have little to do with OCD itself, and that may not be found in different groups of subjects studied somewhere else.

With all these warnings in mind, you may wonder why we bother to review this topic at all. One of the most compelling reasons is that a particular finding does seem to be turning into a fact: the specific benefits for OCD of a particular type of drug that affects one specific brain hormone, or neurotransmitter, *serotonin*.

Serotonergic Drugs in OCD

There will be more on this subject in a later chapter, so it's not covered in its entirety here. But it is important that you first understand one key element: the nature of "brain hormones," or what are more usually called *neurotransmitters*. These are chemicals that nerve cells secrete to stimulate receptors on other nerve cells. They are the means by which one nerve cell communicates with another. The nerve cells connect with each other at contact points called *synapses;* at these synapses, the cells are still separated by microscopic gaps called *(synaptic clefts)*. But one nerve cell can bridge the gap to the next by secreting a neurotransmitter, which diffuses across the gap and stimulates receptors on the other side. Neurotransmitters have names like serotonin, norepinephrine, dopamine, gamma-aminobutyric acid, and many others—including many which have not yet been named or identified. Most medications for mental disorders seem to affect one or another of these neurotransmitters.

Basically, the finding that makes neurotransmitters important to OCD has been that one particular drug—clomipramine (brand name: Anafranil)—relieves OCD symptoms to a degree that other closely related drugs do not. This is surprising. In most mental illnesses, it has been difficult to show consistent superiority of one "active" drug over another; mostly the advantages of an active drug are apparent only in contrast to an inactive (placebo) treatment. When two active drugs are compared, the effects are generally very close to each other in degree. Or if one study shows a superiority of one drug over the other, another study may not, or may even show the opposite. However, in OCD the situation has been different. Clomipramine has consistently come out better than placebo, where such similar drugs as imipramine (Tofranil) and desipramine (Pertofrane, Norpramin) have not. Furthermore, some direct comparisons of clomipramine with other "active" antidepressant drugs have also shown clomipramine superior.

In the battle against depression, clomipramine comes out as an effective, but not an outstandingly superior, antidepressant drug. The same is true of one other drug, fluvoxamine—the only other drug to have shown consistently good evidence for antiobsessive effects. Both these drugs work better than another perfectly good antidepressant, desipramine, in OCD.

So far, the only apparent difference between the OCD-effective drugs and other antidepressants is that clomipramine and fluvoxamine have very strong effects on the neurotransmitter serotonin. (The drugs imipramine and desipramine have lesser effects on serotonin and stronger effects on another neurotransmitter, norepinephrine.) Clomipramine and fluvoxamine are among the most potent drugs available for suppressing the ability of nerve cells to reabsorb serotonin that has been secreted into the synaptic cleft. Remember that reabsorption *inactivates* secreted serotonin. This means that making it harder for nerve cells to reabsorb serotonin will at least temporarily *increase* the effects of serotonin.

This leads to the "serotonin hypothesis" of OCD, which is what a lot of biological research in OCD has been about. The serotonin hypothesis suggests that there is "something wrong" with nerve cell transmission involving serotonin in individuals with OCD. Some researchers go further and suggest that there is some kind of deficiency in serotonin or in the responsiveness to serotonin in those with OCD. That would explain why drugs that increase serotonin function might counteract compulsive behavior. However, this seemingly logical deduction may be misleading, since many other nerve cell events happen as a result of inhibited serotonin reabsorption, and some of these may involve changes in the opposite direction. This is why we limit ourselves to suggesting only that something is wrong with serotonin in OCD individuals.

The next question to consider is whether there is any other evidence—besides the response of OCD to serotonergic drugs—to support this idea.

Is OCD a Disease of Serotonin?

Bear in mind that with current technology there is not yet a way to measure levels of serotonin or observe serotonin in action in the living human brain. As mentioned earlier in this chapter, all the ways to evaluate serotonergic function in humans—with and without OCD—are indirect. Still, the goal is to determine whether OCD patients have different measures of serotonergic function than healthy individuals, as the serotonin hypothesis predicts.

One such indirect measure is the level of serotonin in the blood platelets. Platelets are blood particles involved in clotting that have little to do with nerve cells, but that are easy to obtain by drawing a sample of blood. Platelets absorb serotonin in a way similar to nerve cells, and may therefore be a *model* for this aspect of nerve cell function. One group of researchers measured platelet serotonin and found lower serotonin levels in the platelets of OCD patients than in normal control subjects. Another group could not reproduce this same finding, but did find that the sicker OCD patients had lower platelet serotonin levels than the healthier OCD patients. So, at least two studies suggest that lower platelet serotonin levels have something to do with OCD.

Another approach has been to examine the levels of the serotonin breakdown product, 5-hydroxyindoleacetic acid (5-HIAA), in the spinal fluid. This "by-product" of serotonin breakdown is an indirect measure of the rate at which serotonin is being formed in the brain. It may be another way to estimate serotonin activity in individuals, but in a manner opposite to what you might expect. When serotonin activity is *high,* the nervous system tries to compensate by gearing down the production of serotonin, thereby lowering 5-HIAA. If serotonin activity is too low, it reacts by stepping up the production of serotonin, raising 5-HIAA. One study found 5-HIAA to be higher in OCD patients than in the normal population (as the theory would predict); another study could not reproduce this finding.

Despite such differences in findings, it has been relatively rare for other researchers to find results that exactly *oppose* those that the first researchers reported: that is to say, in general one group doesn't find a particular measure of serotonin too high, and another too low, in OCD patients. Perhaps this in itself is cause for encouragement.

If drugs that work for OCD do so because of their effects on serotonin, you might think to look at how measures of serotonin function are affected by these drugs. Do patients who show stronger effects of a given drug on serotonin function also show better effects of the drug on their OCD?

Clomipramine reduces serotonin in the blood platelets and also reduces 5-HIAA (the serotonin breakdown product) in the spinal fluid. These findings may seem contrary to what you would expect—that clomipramine should *increase* serotonin effects, boosting the levels of serotonin in OCD patients to the levels of healthy people—but they can be understood with a little thought. Clomipramine blocks the ability of platelets to absorb serotonin from the blood, so they end up with less measurable serotonin. At the same time, by inhibiting the reabsorption of serotonin by the nerve cells, clomipramine *increases* the activity of serotonin which has been secreted into the synaptic cleft. The nervous system reacts to this increased serotonin activity by reducing the production of serotonin, which reduces the levels of the serotonin by-product, 5-HIAA. If this seems complicated to you, that's probably an accurate perception of the situation! It may be less confusing if you forget about how clomipramine should increase or decrease a given measure of serotonin, and just remember that it does have a measurable effect.

The two measurable effects of clomipramine on serotonin—decrease of platelet serotonin and decrease of spinal fluid 5-HIAA—*have* been found to correlate with antiobsessive effects of the drug. That is to say, patients experiencing greater clomipramine effects on serotonin function did have better results. Again, the suggestion is supported that antiobsessive effects are related to its effects on serotonin.

Yet another way of testing the serotonin hypothesis of OCD is to look at the effects of other drugs, drugs that affect serotonin in different ways than clomipramine and fluvoxamine. One drug that has attracted interest is called m-chlorophenylpiperazine (mCPP); this drug directly stimulates serotonin receptors on the nerve cells, which should mean increasing serotonin activity. Another is metergoline; this drug blocks serotonin receptors. In one study, mCPP *aggravated* obsessive compulsive symptoms while metergoline *relieved* them. Does this seem contrary to what you would expect from what we have said so far? If so, you have been paying good attention! However, in biological psychiatry it is often possible to explain findings that are opposite to what you would expect. For one thing, the nervous system tries to offset any outside disturbance (such as that caused by a drug) by making a change in the opposite direction at some other point in the chain of effects. One example is the way clomipramine causes reduction of "serotonin turnover" or 5-HIAA. Another may be a reduction of serotonin receptor sensitivity (down regulation) in response to increased levels of serotonin. In any case, other studies have failed to find an aggravation of OCD symptoms with mCPP. Maybe this was a result of one study using intravenous injections of mCPP, while the other gave mCPP by mouth. Or it may just be another example of the principle that "one finding doesn't make a fact." No one really knows the truth about these matters yet.

If you find all this confusing, you are also getting an important point: that the serotonin hypothesis of OCD has not led to simple predictions that have been easily proven or disproven. Nevertheless, the serotonin hypothesis is important, if only because it has turned attention toward a certain type of drug as promising for OCD. These "serotonergic" drugs are being studied intensively for OCD, much more than other drugs that don't affect serotonin. So far, this approach seems to be yielding fruit. Let's hope that researchers are on the right track! It may yet turn out that drugs overlooked because they have nothing to do with serotonin could nevertheless be very helpful for OCD sufferers.

Brain Structure and Metabolism in OCD

Serotonin is not the only lead that researchers have been following in their search for biological abnormalities associated with OCD. A very interesting group of studies have started to look at specific *areas* of the brain and how they function.

A group at UCLA first used a technique called Positron Emission Tomography (PET) to look at the metabolism of glucose in different parts of the brain. They compared OCD patients, depressed patients, and those with no psychiatric disorders. The group found specific abnormalities in OCD— increased metabolic rates in areas called the left orbital gyrus (part of the cortex in the front of the brain) and the caudate (part of the so-called basal ganglia). These abnormalities were not present in the depressed patients or in the non-psychiatric group. They also found that successful drug treatment of the OCD symptoms changed these abnormal metabolic rates, whereas the rates did not change when drug treatment was unsuccessful.

Another group of researchers, at the National Institute of Mental Health, used a technique known as Computed Tomography (CT) to look at the size of different areas of the brain in OCD patients and in non-psychiatric subjects. They found in OCD patients a decrease in the size of one area—the caudate—which the UCLA group had found to have an abnormal metabolic rate in OCD individuals. In other words, two quite different techniques seemed to be pointing in the same direction.

Unfortunately, another PET study from a different center failed to duplicate this finding with the caudate. So did another study using Magnetic Resonance Imaging (MRI) to measure the size of different brain structures. But the second PET study did show abnormalities in the frontal cortex, as the UCLA group had found. Recently the NIMH researchers reported similar findings, making it seem more likely that it may be a *fact* that functioning of the frontal cortex is disturbed in OCD.

All of this still doesn't add up to an understanding of how different areas of the brain play roles in generating the symptoms of OCD. Still, more studies may produce more consistent findings, which would form the basis of more solid theory. This is a particularly exciting area to follow, because new technology is making it possible to look at more and more aspects of the living human brain.

OCD and "Biological Markers" for Other Disorders

A number of biological tests were developed first in studying other mental disorders, such as depression, and then applied to OCD. These include the dexamethasone suppression test (DST) and the sleep electroencephalogram (EEG).

The dexamethasone suppression test has been the most studied. This is a hormonal test. It involves giving the patient a small dose of a synthetic steroid hormone, dexamethasone, and measuring the effect of this dexamethasone on the patient's own secretion of the natural steroid hormone, cortisol. Cortisol is important to the immune system and is elevated by stress. To the brain, the small amount of dexamethasone seems like a very high level of steroid; therefore, the brain acts through the pituitary gland to turn off production of cortisol in the adrenals for a while. (This is another example of a negative feedback process, like the reduction of 5-HIAA by clomipramine.) After dexamethasone, it is usual for blood cortisol to fall to low levels for the next 24 hours. However, in some depressed people these cortisol levels start to climb back up earlier than in normal control subjects. This is called abnormal escape, or non-suppression, of cortisol from dexamethasone. It is uncommon in healthy people but quite common in depressed people, of whom perhaps two-thirds may show abnormal DST results. The DST is also often abnormal in certain other psychiatric disorders. One of these disorders seems to be OCD. However, many OCD sufferers are also depressed—at least some of the time—and it now seems likely that it is mostly the more depressed OCD patients who show abnormal DSTs. In other words, a DST result may say more about whether or not you are depressed than whether or not you have OCD.

Something like this may also be true of the sleep electroencephalogram. This test is conducted while you sleep all night in a laboratory where your brain waves (the EEG) can be continuously monitored. Throughout the night, the normal person moves through different stages of sleep in a typical way. The depressed person often shows specific abnormalities in this sleep cycle—for example, starting the first episode of Rapid Eye Movement (REM, or dreaming sleep) sooner than expected. OCD patients may show some of these same abnormalities in their sleep patterns. But again, the results may have more to do with depression than with OCD.

In addition to what has been described in this chapter, there are other tests that have been used to compare OCD patients to patients with other diagnoses or with normal subjects. These include the waking EEG, the evoked potential (which measures the EEG response to a specific stimulus such as light), blood types, levels of the vitamin B-12, levels of thyroid hormones, levels of the hormone prolactin, and response of hormones like prolactin and growth hormone to specific drugs. More such biological measures are undoubtedly under study and will be heard of soon. You'll find little detail about these here because they have not yet gotten beyond the point of isolated and sometimes contradictory findings. This situation may change, but when you read about some new finding, keep in mind one general principle: a single finding doesn't make a fact. The same finding must be repeatedly found by other research groups before it can be thought of as fact.

There is one last area, only partly in the biological realm, that deserves some more attention: family patterns of OCD.

The Genetics of OCD

This is of interest from a psychological as well as a biological perspective. Much interest in family studies has been stimulated by the suspicion that OCD is hereditary. The early studies did not show as much OCD in the relatives of OCD patients as, say, other studies show depression in the relatives of depressed patients. However, this may be largely a result of the tendency of OCD sufferers to hide their problems from others. You may have relatives with OCD that you do not even know about, especially if they belonged to an earlier generation. As more and more OCD sufferers "come out of the closet," it becomes clearer and clearer that OCD does run in families—sometimes to a striking extent—where several members are affected in one way or another. Just asking an OCD patient which first-degree relatives (parents, siblings, children) he or she *knows* to have OCD may give a "familial prevalence" of 20 to 30 percent; directly interviewing all relatives would certainly raise this prevalence still higher.

Sometimes an OCD patient may have a parent who engages in obsessive-compulsive behavior without seeming particularly bothered by it. This makes the parent's problem seem more like the personality disorder discussed in the previous chapter than like OCD itself. Still, the parent may have a mild form of OCD, not severe enough to bother him or her, what might be called "subclinical" OCD. Relatives of an OCD patient may also have clear-cut OCD, but of a completely *different* type from the patient's. The father may be a checker and the son a washer, or vice versa. This raises doubts about whether the son could have "learned" obsessive-compulsive behavior from his father, as opposed to inheriting the predisposition to it genetically.

Another way of examining this issue is to look at twins, who may be either identical (monozygotic) and share the same genes, or fraternal (dizygotic) and share no more of the same genes than siblings who are not twins. As in other diseases with a hereditary component, if one of an identical twin pair has OCD, the other twin is much more likely also to have OCD than is the case with a fraternal twin pair. Of course, "identical" twins may be treated more alike, and thus upbringing may be a factor; that's why researchers often seek out twins who have been adopted away early in life and raised separately. Such studies have yet to be done in OCD, though in other mental illnesses they have tended to support the idea of a strong genetic factor.

Obviously, much more research needs to be done before biological bases for OCD are really understood. If this chapter helps you read about new research findings in a more understanding—and skeptical—way, it will have accomplished its aim. Meanwhile, don't hold your breath waiting for a "breakthrough" that will solve the problem for you; and don't discourage yourself by thinking that you *need* to await a scientific breakthrough either. There is a lot that can be done to help solve these problems long before they are fully understood. Many "biological" illnesses can benefit greatly from such "psychological" treatments as we are about to describe.

Summary

It is dangerous to oversimplify the cause of OCD as either biological or psychological. There are probably multiple biological and psychological factors that act together to determine who gets OCD and how severe it is.

In considering reports of research findings, beware of taking a single finding as representing a fact. Only repeated findings of the same sort by different researchers can establish whether a new fact has been discovered. Especially in mental health, where experiments are difficult to conduct and control, it is commonplace for different researchers to get different answers to the same questions.

One finding that has been confirmed repeatedly in the area of OCD is the effectiveness of drugs that affect serotonin, and possibly their superiority to drugs that affect other neurotransmitters such as norepinephrine. This has led to the serotonin hypothesis of the biological basis of OCD. Researchers have tried to find further support for this serotonin hypothesis by looking at several indirect measures of serotonin function in OCD patients—such as blood platelet serotonin levels and cerebrospinal fluid levels of the serotonin breakdown product, 5-HIAA. These studies have yielded some positive findings but no facts so far.

Other studies have looked at the structure and activity of specific areas of the brain in OCD. There may be abnormalities in the frontal orbital cortex and possibly the caudate nucleus of OCD sufferers. Still other studies have looked at "biological markers" associated with mood disorders, like the dexamethasone suppression test and the sleep electroencephalogram. These may be abnormal in OCD patients mainly when they are also severely depressed. None of these statements yet amounts to a fact either.

Finally, there are indications that OCD does run in families, and may be in part hereditary. It is particularly striking that OCD may take very different forms in parent and child.

4

Learned Bases for OCD

Professionals have developed three main theories to explain Obsessive Compulsive Disorder (OCD). One is called *psychodynamic* (or psychoanalytic) theory; one *cognitive* theory; and another *behavioral* (or learning) theory. This book draws mainly on behavioral theory, which is based on observable actions and reactions for its strategies. Cognitive theory derived from behavioral theory but is not yet as well developed or studied. Behavioral and cognitive theories are quite different from the third group, psychodynamic concepts. Still, the theories are often compatible with one another.

The real focus of this chapter—and of the book—is behavioral theory. But first it is important to understand the alternative theories of OCD. Psychodynamic theory is the basis for the "talk therapy" most present-day psychotherapists practice. Most people who have sought treatment for OCD have already received this type of therapy with varying degrees of success. It's less likely that you've encountered cognitive theory in treatment, since this is a field that has yet to be carefully researched. Nevertheless, cognitive theory deserves attention as a potential source of future treatment for OCD. This chapter will briefly explore all three groups of theories.

Psychodynamic Theory

Classical Freudian psychoanalysts have viewed obsessions and compulsions as psychological defenses against anxious feelings originating in early childhood. Those anxious feelings, according to the theory, stem specifically from angry or sexual impulses experienced by the child. The impulses were unacceptable to the child's conscience and therefore were rarely acted upon. But since they couldn't be acted upon directly, they provoked considerable anxiety and defensive thoughts and behaviors.

For example, a child might have developed a preoccupation with harming someone or with dirt as a defensive way of distracting him- or herself from other more significant and more disturbing angry thoughts. These more disturbing impulses therefore remain repressed in the unconscious part of his or her mind. The new preoccupations replace the repressed impulses. Generally, most psychodynamic theorists do not distinguish between defensive roles played by obsessions and by compulsions: both are considered defense mechanisms designed to take attention away from the true anxiety-causing issues.

Psychodynamic theorists explain the magical thinking and the indecision often characteristic of OCD as a result of the person's efforts to return (regress) to an earlier stage of childhood development. If you feel conflict and anxiety over sexual issues, for instance, you put yourself back to the mindstate of a child who has not yet become aware of sexual impulses. It's not a conscious move, but it is a way to dodge the problem.

Other symptoms of OCD are also explained as defensive strategies developed to avoid internal emotional conflicts.

Some defense mechanisms thought to be common among OCD sufferers include:

1. "reaction formation": transforming an unwanted feeling, like anger at your mother, into another seemingly opposite symptom, like worrying that she'll die in an accident. This can lead to rituals to magically prevent the new fear from happening.
2. "isolation": disconnecting an idea from its associated emotions (for example, anger). That might allow an individual to obsess about stabbing someone he or she loves without even feeling angry at the person.
3. "undoing": compulsive behaviors such as repeating or checking as an effort to remove angry or sexual feelings that make the doer uncomfortable.
4. "displacement": transferring conflicted feelings or anxiety from one area, such as having inappropriate sexual feelings, to another less emotionally charged one, such as getting a disease from a person.

Some theorists known as ego psychologists follow these psychodynamic beliefs about the origin of the disorder—that is, they accept Freud's idea that anxiety from uncomfortable childhood impulses lingers and must be defended against—but they choose to focus on the obsessive-compulsive's insecurity too much and helplessness. This distinguishes them from psychodynamic theorists, who focus their attention on early conflicts and defense mechanisms. Still, the general orientation of all these theorists is to attribute OCD symptoms to unconscious processes.

The different versions of psychodynamic theory have led to treatments in which the therapist tries mainly to interpret the patient's unconscious conflicts. This involves having the patient discuss freely his or her thoughts, feelings, and behaviors, and having the analyst comment on their possible importance and meaning with respect to early unconscious conflicts. The hope is that once the patient recognizes those buried and uncomfortable feelings, he or she can address the real issues instead of diverting that energy and anxiety to the substitute rituals. Freud exhorted psychoanalysts to urge their patients to give up their rituals, once interpretations were made and accepted by the patient. Although such psychoanalytic methods are usually long-term treatments often involving years of two or three weekly sessions, several short-term psychodynamic treatment methods have recently been developed and are practiced by many psychotherapists. Most notable of these is Peter Sifneos' "Short Term Anxiety-Provoking Psychotherapy" (STAPP). This involves identifying the patient's main underlying conflict and interpreting his or her present difficulties in light of this main conflict, even if the patient may not yet be fully aware of the conflictual issues. Initial reports of this treatment's effectiveness with carefully selected (and possibly only mildly symptomatic) patients have been positive, but this approach has not yet been tested in comparison with other methods.

Cognitive Theory

Some writers have proposed that "cognitive" or mental processes (learning, logical thinking, and awareness) may play an important role in the genesis of OCD. These theorists differ from psychoanalytical thinkers by focusing more on conscious thoughts than on unconscious conflicts. They note, for example, that many people with OCD seem to engage in "black-or-white" thinking in which they have difficulty seeing or tolerating the "grey" areas of uncertainty. These sufferers prefer to determine whether a situation is completely safe or completely dangerous for instance, and appear to have considerable difficulty with the notion of "pretty safe" or "probably not dangerous." The pattern of accepting only extremes is seen as evidence that many OCD patients have trouble accepting uncertainty.

Most cognitive theorists believe that obsessions and compulsions are the by-product of unreasonable assumptions of danger and distorted perceptions of one's ability to cope with that danger. Irrational beliefs thought to be held by obsessive-compulsive persons include the following:

1. the importance of perfection in oneself.
2. the belief that one should be punished if he or she fails to achieve these perfectionistic ideals.
3. the idea that magical rituals can prevent catastrophes.
4. the idea that certain thoughts or feelings are dangerous because they can lead to disastrous consequences, and that one should be punished for having such dangerous thoughts.

According to a cognitive model, these mistaken beliefs exaggerate one's perception of danger, and therefore lead to anxiety, guilt, and other unpleasant emotions. If people also fear they cannot cope with the danger when it arises, they feel uncertain and helpless. They may adopt magical rituals to reduce these feelings, since they lack other coping methods.

Another version of cognitive theory proprosed by Drs. Foa and Kozak focuses on specific networks of information encoded in memory. All people have some fears and have stored information about their fears in memory. Each fear network contains information about disturbing cues, reactions of fear or discomfort, and the meanings attached to the cues and the reactions. Theorists who advance this cognitive theory believe that the information networks of OCD sufferers contain mistaken estimates of threat or danger. They also suggest that sufferers are especially afraid of the specific danger they expect (perhaps because of scary early experiences or teachings associated with that danger). For example, a person who had head lice as a child and endured unpleasant treatments and teasing from other children may become especially prone to protecting him- or herself, or his or her children, from similar experiences. Similarly, a child taught by austere nuns that he or she might go to hell for thinking "bad" thoughts may be predisposed to fear dire consequences for sexual or blasphemous fantasies in adulthood. Thus the person overreacts to the perceived threat, both in thought and in action. Over time, the reactions become ingrained and difficult to change.

Treatment, according to this theory, is based on altering these elements of the fear network. People with OCD are gradually exposed to their feared situations, and led to observe that the feared danger does not occur. An alternative method is to show the sufferer that the danger feared is not as calamitous as imagined, so the sufferer becomes less sensitive to the possibility of its occurrence. These methods are based on the observation that people with OCD tend to assume a situation is dangerous, unless they have specific evidence that it is "safe." Preventative measures such as rituals stop the situation from occurring (in the sufferer's mind), so there is never a chance to see whether it would have been "safe" anyway. And even rituals don't guarantee complete safety, since they must be repeated. These ideas are addressed in cognitive treatment, as rituals are gradually eliminated.

Cognitive theories of OCD are intuitively appealing for their ability to describe the disorder and to explain some of the phenomena commonly observed. As yet, they have been tested in only very limited ways, however. Little evidence exists to support or refute their validity. Eventually, cognitive therapeutic strategies may be added to behavioral therapy, an approach based on the most solid clinical evidence available. For now, behavior therapy alone remains the surest and most finely tuned approach. It is the approach espoused by this book, and will be discussed in greater detail in the following chapter.

Behavioral Theory

Behavioral theories of OCD have been more explicit than psychodynamic theories in defining obsessive and compulsive symptoms and their functions, as well as the goals of treatment. Ideas about how obsessions and compulsions are acquired are not well developed by behavioral theorists, although some ideas have been advanced and are discussed below. By contrast, the maintenance of these symptoms, once established, is more easily accounted for by behavioral theory, as we shall show.

To understand the tenets of behavioral theory, it helps to recall the definition of OCD as discussed in Chapter 2. Obsessions are viewed as mental events (such as thoughts or images) or behavioral actions that increase discomfort; compulsions are defined as behaviors or thoughts that are carried out to reduce the discomfort provoked by the obsessions.

One widely accepted behavioral model for understanding how obsessive-compulsive symptoms are acquired and maintained is the *two-stage* theory. According to this theory, the learning of fear and avoidance involves two distinct stages. In the first stage, a non-disturbing object (or thought), such as a toilet seat or scissors, appears in the context of an event that produces pain or other unpleasant reactions, such as an illness or loss of a loved one. This pairing might happen once or several times, and it results in an association between the neutral event and the unpleasant emotion. In the second stage, because of the aversive nature of the event, the individual develops behaviors or thoughts that help avoid the disturbing situation. Often, these patterns of avoidance include the associated object as well. These responses persist because they reduce the unpleasant emotional state. This process is called *negative* reinforcement because the avoidance temporarily *removes* a frightening or painful experience. (Positive reinforcement, by contrast, is the *addition* of a desirable reward for certain behavior.)

The person may come to associate other usually neutral cues—words, images, thoughts, concrete objects—with the first frightening event. These associated situations acquire equal ability to provoke unpleasant emotions (especially fear, guilt, and shame), which the person tries to escape or avoid whenever possible. For example, once scissors are associated with the fear of stabbing someone, any sharp object similar to scissors (knives, awls, screwdrivers, etc.) may become associated with this fear.

Because of this secondary conditioning process, the original source of fear is often obscured and the anxiety associated with it may become diffused into a more general feeling of discomfort. An example of this is the case of a man who originally experienced fear during a radioactive spill in a medical laboratory. He began to wash and clean extensively. He also avoided the lab, as well as the people who had been present at the spill, and the places where they went, for fear that they might still be radioactive. Years later, even after moving away from the city, his fear continued to focus on the places where the people had gone. In fact, the fear had generalized widely to the entire city where the spill had occurred. At the time he began treatment, he was not aware of any fear of radioactivity, and indeed could go into areas in his new lab where radioactive products were used. He feared and avoided only the city of the original spill, as well as every object and person that came from there.

In addition to the avoidance responses typical of people who have phobias, OCD sufferers develop compulsions or rituals to cope with their anxiety. These compulsions persist despite their seeming absurdity precisely because they reduce or avert unpleasant emotional reactions. For people with OCD, the relationship between specific compulsions and the situation(s) that provoke them is only sometimes clear. It is easy to see why a woman whose child ate rat poison and had to be taken to the hospital would become highly sensitive to chemicals or poisons. Washing and cleaning rituals, as well as repeatedly calling the poison control hotline, seem very logically related to the source of her fear. Similarly, praying rituals may reduce the fear of having committed a mortal sin, and mentally listing the day's events may offset the chance that something terribly important will be forgotten. These rituals are all logically related to the type of fear experienced.

Other rituals can be harder to explain. Some seem to be acquired by chance, merely because they led to a reduction in fear or other aversive emotions on a particular occasion. For example, repeating a specific numerical sequence or set of phrases in order to neutralize a bad thought about someone dying in an auto accident is not a logical response. However, if relief occurred by chance when a particular set of numbers was said, then a person might acquire a belief that the numbers actually help prevent harmful accidents. The more a person uses a ritual, the more convinced he or she may become that only this specific behavior can reduce discomfort. Such rituals are much like superstitions.

It is not surprising that people with OCD can acquire *multiple rituals*, particularly in response to intrusive disturbing thoughts. Most people with phobias can try to avoid the feared situation (for example, heights, dogs, social events) to reduce or prevent anxiety. But for those whose feared situations are mental ideas (for example, of being homosexual), images (for example, of Christ's penis), or impulses (for example, to stab one's child with a knife), avoidance is difficult or impossible. Rituals to undo the unwanted idea come to seem essential to control anxiety or guilt. Further, even for those whose fears center on concrete objects, such as chemicals or germ infected places, avoidance is often impossible because of *generalization.* This refers to the spreading of fear to other objects in close or even remote association with the original feared object. Contamination "travels": a washer might picture a co-worker who did not wash her hands after using the bathroom touching the bathroom door handle, then the office door, and then her desk and all its contents. Other unsuspecting workers touch places that she touched and unwittingly spread contamination further. Once a fear becomes generalized, it requires more active defensive maneuvers than mere avoidance, and thus washing and cleaning rituals are developed.

The ideas described above seem to explain—according to the behavioral model—how OCD fears spread and how fear and rituals persist despite an unreasonableness apparent even to the sufferer. But many people with OCD cannot recall an initial aversive or threatening event that led directly to the onset of obsessions. Many do remember that these symptoms began during a very stressful period. Researchers have suggested that the general fear or tension accompanying periods of stress may render people more susceptible to fears or obsessions that have a special significance for them. In a sense, stress may lower the tolerance threshold, so that "normal" fearful ideas that occur randomly can more easily become obsessive thoughts.

Almost everyone has some strange or potentially upsetting thoughts, images, or impulses from time to time. Often these are taboo aggressive or religious thoughts (for example, imagining knifing one's grandmother or picturing Christ's penis) which people are taught early to see as unacceptable. Under stress these ideas may develop more easily into obsessions that provoke fear, avoidance, and rituals. Research has at least confirmed that once a person develops OCD symptoms, stressful life situations almost invariably make them worse.

In sum, behavioral theory suggests that people learn to associate certain objects or situations with fear or discomfort and use rituals to reduce discomfort that cannot be avoided altogether. This theory explains how obsessions and compulsions persist over so many years despite their senselessness, although it is not always clear how the OCD symptoms began. Treatments based on this theory have proven quite successful and are described in later chapters.

Explaining the Onset of OCD

The above discussion of psychodynamic, cognitive, and behavioral theories tries to explain *how* the seemingly peculiar symptoms of OCD persist despite the fact that sufferers know the rituals are unreasonable. But the question of *why* some people are afflicted with the disorder, whereas others are not, is only partly answered. The pairing of a neutral situation with an unusually unpleasant experience (recall the mother whose child ate rat poison), part of the "two-stage" behavioral model, could certainly explain some of the initial fear and its association with related objects or situations. But not all persons with OCD remember any aversive experience that led to their obsessions and rituals. Nor do all people who have such experiences develop OCD. Who, then, is likely to develop OCD? What characterizes sufferers and explains the initial development of this disorder? The suggestions offered here in answer to these questions are just that—suggestions. Some are supported by research, whereas others are not and must be considered merely speculative. In truth, no one really knows why some people develop the disorder and others do not.

As is clear from the previous chapter, there is considerable evidence that genetic factors play some role in the onset of OCD. Still, these factors cannot account for all or even most cases. For example, the parents of OCD individuals rarely have OCD themselves, but often do have obsessive traits or other types of psychiatric illness such as depression or anxiety. And yet, some obsessive-compulsives come from families without evidence of any psychiatric disorder. Several biological factors were identified and discussed earlier (see Chapter 3), but again the evidence is not overwhelming. Further, some of the biological features associated with OCD may, in fact, be a result of psychological experiences. For example, serotonin, a chemical found in the brain, appears to be important in OCD. But disturbances in serotonin function may be a *result* of the experience of obsessions and compulsions rather than its *cause.*

Many investigators have hypothesized that child-rearing practices may contribute to the development of OCD. For example, psychoanalytic theorists suggest that toilet training procedures for those who later developed OCD may be too harsh or rigid. This idea has not been supported by evidence. Characteristics of parents sometimes associated with offspring who develop this disorder are perfectionism, and denial or avoidance of aggressive and sexual urges. But not all children of parents who are *perfectionistic* and *rigid* in their standards, or who teach their children according to moralistic, guilt-inducing beliefs, develop OCD. There are numerous examples of individuals who develop obsessions and compulsions who do not come from such families. In most cases it seems clear that parents should not hold themselves responsible for the development of this disorder in their children. Still, most mental health professionals would agree that non-judgmental, flexible attitudes in parents are probably more helpful than harsh and rigid ones.

There is some evidence that family members who are highly *critical* of a relative who develops OCD are likely to impede the person's progress in therapy. Similarly, family members who believe that their relative could control the OCD symptoms if only he or she tried are also likely to hinder the person's long-term benefit from treatment. But again, this does not mean that criticism or a lack of understanding can lead to the development of the disorder. Perhaps these parents are merely reacting to their own frustration at being unable to help a son, daughter, or other family member combat this bewildering psychological problem. Difficult though it may be to secure, however, family members' support may play an important part in helping individuals with OCD overcome their symptoms.

There is some evidence that OCD patients tend to be more *religious* than other individuals, although clearly not all religious people are obsessive or compulsive to a degree that interferes with their functioning. *Guilt* appears to be a common feature of people with this disorder, but research has pinpointed guilt as a common factor in other kinds of anxiety disorders as well. No evidence exists that excessive guilt is specific to OCD.

Another speculation is that OCD often begins during early or middle adolescence, when relationships with peers, and particularly the opposite sex, become very important. Perhaps obsessions and compulsions serve to prevent adolescents who are very *anxious or unskilled in social activities* from having to attend social events. This idea is similar to some of the psychodynamic concepts discussed earlier in this chapter about OCD symptoms as defenses against unconscious feelings or ideas people don't like to admit. Again, there is not sufficient evidence to argue in favor of this idea, although it is true that many OCD individuals have social difficulties. However, this may be more a consequence of the debilitating symptoms than their cause. Further, many do not appear to have problems with friendships, dating, or marriage, and report being happy in these areas of their lives.

Summary

There are three different approaches to explaining the origin and persistence of obsessive-compulsive symptoms: psychodynamic, cognitive, and behavioral theories. The bases for these theories differ substantially. Psychodynamic theory suggests that obsessions and compulsions originate in angry and/or sexual impulses during childhood. Cognitive theories presume that fearful behaviors are determined by the way people think. OCD sufferers are thought to have particular types of beliefs and patterns of thought that lead them to engage in obsessive thinking and compulsive rituals.Behavioral theory is derived from an assumption that OCD symptoms, like other fearful behavior, is learned from experience. The symptoms are maintained, according to behaviorists, because escape from and avoidance of feared situations produces relief, and that helps to reinforce the fearful pattern.

Perhaps the only answer we can give with conviction about the onset of OCD is that *many factors are involved,* and that no one can yet predict who will develop the disorder. Of course, if no one can predict its onset, no one can yet prevent it either. Much can still be done, however, in the attempt to alleviate the symptoms and their unfortunate side effects of depression, anxiety, and poor social functioning.

5

Research Findings on Behavioral Treatments for Obsessions and Compulsions

As the name suggests, Obsessive Compulsive Disorder is almost always marked by two distinct groups of symptoms: 1) obsessions that provoke discomfort and avoidance of certain situations, and 2) compulsive actions that attempt to reduce this discomfort. Obsessive fears and compulsive behaviors or thoughts are closely linked. In order to reduce these symptoms effectively, it is important to use treatment methods that address *both* the obsessions and the compulsions simultaneously. Treatments that focus only on obsessions or on compulsions have proven considerably less effective in treating OCD than methods that address both symptom areas. Which procedures should you apply to each of the symptoms? This chapter is designed to give you an overview of the methods studied so far and the results achieved with them. In the next several chapters, we will discuss how to use the most effective of these methods with your own obsessive and compulsive symptoms.

Early Exposure Treatment Methods

Several methods were tested in the 1960s and 1970s for the treatment of obsessive fears. All aimed to reduce anxiety through exposure—either direct or indirect—to some aspect of the feared situation.

One procedure explored was *systematic desensitization*, developed by Joseph Wolpe in the late 1950s to treat specific types of phobias (such as fear of heights). Researchers thought it might prove useful in treating OCD patients. Desensitization consists of three parts. First, a patient develops a list of feared situations that have a central theme, such as contamination from chemicals, and arranges the list according to the degree of fear each circumstance evokes. Second, the patient is taught techniques for relaxing each muscle group (for example, the muscles of the forearm) very deeply, so that with practice, he or she can relax quickly and at will. Third, the patient is asked to relax deeply while picturing him- or herself in one of the mildly disturbing situations from the list. The patient alternates between imagining the scene and relaxing until fear associated with that situation is reduced to a very low level. Then the next scene is imagined in the same way, and so on up to the hierarchy of feared situations. Desensitization may be conducted either in the imagination as described above ("imagined" desensitization), or in the actual feared situation (*"in vivo"* desensitization). *In vivo* desensitization combines relaxation techniques with increasing doses of the feared objects or circumstances themselves.

Both methods of desensitization—imagined and *in vivo*—have been used very successfully to treat phobias over the past three decades. However, they were not found very effective in the treatment of obsessive fears. Only about 30 to

40 percent of those who were treated with imaginal desensitization saw lasting improvement; the success rate for desensitization to real situations was somewhat higher, but still unsatisfactory. The problem appears to be that this method is very time-consuming, sometimes requiring 200 or more treatment sessions for those with multiple obsessive fears. Furthermore, those with extensive and long-standing obsessive symptoms remained highly anxious between treatment sessions, and continued to do their rituals. Not surprisingly, it took a long time for patients to feel even a little better. It took longer yet to convince them that they no longer needed to perform their rituals. Some OCD patients never gave up their compulsions. Systematic desensitization, then, does not seem to be useful for most people with OCD. However, some researchers have shown that it may be helpful for those whose symptoms are of very recent onset—when obsessive fears are not extensive and when rituals are not firmly established habits.

Paradoxical intention is another type of exposure method that has been used to reduce obsessions. Paradoxical intention involves asking the obsessive person to try to *increase* the frequency or intensity of his or her problematic thoughts. Often, attempts are made to include humor in this process. Thus, a person who fears having run over a pedestrian while driving would be asked to worry continually about having run over a person, and in fact to worry about having run over a whole army of people, leaving a long trail of bodies behind with arms and legs and brightly colored clothes flung every which way.

Although some success has been found using paradoxical intention, overall only about half of the patients in whom it was tested improved substantially. That is, many found that their obsessions did not decrease in frequency or intensity. One group of researchers tried this method with compulsive behaviors. They asked patients to repeat their rituals over and over again, even when they didn't need to, hoping that the compulsions would become so aversive to the patients that they would cease. In fact, all four patients on whom this was tried refused to follow instructions. Interestingly, they improved, although it would be difficult to argue that this paradoxical instruction was successful treatment strategy.

Another very similar procedure—*satiation*—has also been studied. In this procedure, obsessive patients are asked to repeat their feared ideas or thoughts aloud or in writing, again and again for periods of one hour or more. Unfortunately, only a small percentage of people treated in this way have improved according to research studies. In general, both paradoxical intention and satiation have been aimed at reducing obsessive fears alone, without attempting to treat compulsive behaviors. It seems that investigators simply assumed that when obsessive anxiety was reduced, the need to perform rituals would automatically disappear. Probably, obsessive fears did decline somewhat after these treatments, but rituals were still needed to reduce those fears even further. Rituals continued to serve an important, anxiety-reducing function, and could not readily be given up.

Programs of exposure to obsessive fears, then, proved to have only limited effects on those fears for OCD sufferers. The programs—desensitization, paradoxical intention, and satiation—had even less beneficial impact on patients' compulsive acts. Researchers were forced to look elsewhere for an effective method of treating OCD obsessions and compulsions.

Blocking Methods

Another set of treatments investigated falls under the general term of "blocking" methods. Blocking methods attempt to reduce OCD symptoms by preventing, stopping, or punishing either the obsessions or the compulsions or both.

With respect to obsessions, you can see that these strategies use the *opposite* approach of exposure procedures, which seek to prolong the obsession until fear reduces of its own accord. Several successful individual cases have been reported in which patients were given small electrical shocks to the forearm whenever they indicated that they were thinking obsessive thoughts. Similar methods using the snapping of a rubber band on the wrist instead of electric shock have also been tried. In general, these aversive methods have not worked well for obsessive thoughts.

When blocking methods are applied to compulsions, they are intended either to punish the ritual so the patient associates compulsions with pain, or to prevent the ritual altogether and thus break the automatic compulsive habits. In some reported cases, electrical shocks or snaps of a rubber band have been effective in reducing rituals. It's interesting to note that for some other types of psychiatric problems, such as habit reduction (for example, smoking) and inappropriate sexual behavior (for example, exhibitionism), aversion treatment has led to initial improvement. Even in those cases, though, there are high rates of relapse. Of course, these blocking methods are inherently painful and therefore unpleasant treatments. Since there is little evidence of their effectiveness in OCD except in a few cases, and since other highly effective methods have been developed, aversive blocking procedures are not recommended. They have, in fact, been little used in recent years.

Thought-stopping is another blocking technique that has been used with obsessions, as well as compulsions. In this method, the patient is asked to shout the word "stop" after thinking or voicing an obsessive idea. After a little while, the patient merely *says* the word stop, and eventually just thinks it to him- or herself. In a sense, this is like the electric shock or rubber band treatments described above: the need to shout "stop" is an unpleasant consequence that follows an obsessive idea. Although simple and easy to use, this method has produced positive results in only about one-third of those who have tried it. It is possible that thought-stopping could be useful for relieving mental *compulsions* (not obsessions), but researchers have not yet adequately studied this question.

Comparisons of Exposure and Blocking Methods

Exposure methods and blocking methods seem to be equally effective in the treatment of OCD—or, more accurately, equally ineffective. In general, neither method has produced particularly good results in reducing the symptoms of OCD patients. Many of the exposure and blocking procedures ran into problems since they were used to treat *both* obsessive fears and compulsive rituals. Thought-stopping, for example, could be used to interrupt both obsessive thoughts about blaspheming God, and compulsive thoughts such a praying for forgiveness. In this way, both anxiety-increasing ideas (blasphemy) and anxiety-reducing ones (prayer) were blocked. The result was rarely overall improvement. Similarly, exposure methods such as satiation have also been applied equally to obsessive ideas and to compulsive thoughts. This indiscriminate application of exposure and blocking methods to both obsessions and compulsions has been inappropriate, as you'll see below.

Combined Exposure and Blocking Methods

The theories presented in Chapter 4 suggest that obsessions and compulsions have opposite functions with respect to fear or anxiety. Obsessions increase fear, and compulsions reduce it. It seems sensible, then, that these functions should be taken into account when designing methods for treatment. Researcher Victor Meyer did just that in England in 1966. He proposed the simultaneous use of two different approaches—one, gradual prolonged exposure, would be aimed at reducing obsessional ruminations, and another, blocking or "response prevention," would be aimed at reducing compulsive rituals. Meyer stressed that both treatments would be needed *simultaneously* in order to reduce fear and eliminate rituals.

This combined exposure and ritual prevention treatment was first tried with patients who suffered from fears of "contamination" and from washing rituals. Meyer proposed that several hours of daily contact with increasingly disturbing situations—from fingerprints on door handles, say, to "germs" from a public restroom—would be time and exposure enough for fear to reduce. To ensure that patients didn't resort to washing when they first felt fear, the faucets in their hospital rooms were turned off. The nursing staff was asked to continuously monitor their use of water in the hospital restrooms and showers. After all, patients would only benefit if they realized slowly that their feared situations wouldn't hurt them; nothing would be accomplished if they resorted to rituals (washing) to immediately reduce their anxiety. Meyer expected that patients would eventually become accustomed to using public toilets and other feared places. Ideally, the fear would be reduced without the need to resort to extensive washing or cleaning rituals.

Meyer's treatment program was very effective. All of the patients improved: 10 of the 15 patients were considered to be much improved after treatment, and the other five moderately improved. Five to six years later, only two lost their gains and were considered to have relapsed. Not surprisingly, these excellent results generated considerable interest in the type of treatment that Meyer and his staff had employed. A series of studies followed in the 1970s and 1980s in which this combined therapy program was tested in several other treatment centers with large numbers of OCD patients.

The combined exposure and ritual prevention procedure has been studied in England, Holland, Greece, India, Canada, and the United States. The results across all of these studies have been quite consistent: about 65 to 75 percent of those with obsessions and with compulsive rituals have benefitted substantially from the treatment program. Few were completely "cured"—that is, entirely free of obsessions and compulsions. But most found themselves much improved; they were considerably less anxious and felt less compelled to perform their rituals. Participants also benefitted from decreased feelings of depression, and improved work, school, and social functioning, as well as improved family relationships.

Compulsive rituals—even very extensive ones—were quite effectively treated by this combination method. In the vast majority of patients, ritualizing was reduced significantly or even eliminated. The results were less consistent for obsessive thoughts, images, and impulses, and avoidance of feared situations. The frequency and severity of these symptoms improved considerably, but by no means completely for most of those in the treatment program. It seems that reduction in obsessive fear lags somewhat behind improvement in rituals. Apparently, more time than the two or three months allotted by most treatment programs is needed to reduce the obsessive symptoms.

Variants of Exposure Treatments

Various aspects of Meyer's exposure and response prevention therapy program have been studied is recent years. Researchers in England wondered whether the presence of a person who first demonstrated or "modeled" the fearful action would be helpful. They had such a model touch a contaminated object without washing, or perform a routine action like turning off the stove without checking, while the patient watched. The patient was then asked to do the same task. The study findings indicated that the model made little difference in OCD patients' ability to confront the feared situation, or in the amount of fear they felt while engaging in it. Those who observed the model did no better than those who did the tasks alone.

In fact, most patients feel they have already seen other people do these things without ritualizing many times; seeing one more person do it makes little differences to them. Ultimately, they need to do it themselves. Still, a few patients do feel that having someone they trust lead the way is immediately helpful. Modeling, to them, makes the task at hand a little less formidable. In current therapy practice, therefore, most therapists offer to model the exposure situation first. The patient can decide whether or not this would be more helpful than mere instructions.

Length of Exposure

Another much-studied aspect of exposure treatment is its optimal duration. For how long should a person who is afraid of touching public doorknobs stay in contact with this feared object? In general, longer exposure periods have proven more effective than briefer periods: they allow more time for reduction of fear. No one knows what the optimal time period for exposure is, nor exactly when to stop a particular exposure session. For most people, discomfort begins to decline after 30 to 60 minutes, and often it decreases further during the second hour. Therefore, a session of one to two hours is commonly used.

It appears to be important to allow the patient enough time to experience what he or she considers to be a significant decrease in fear by his or her own estimate. By the end of the exposure period, the desire to stop the exposure should be *less* strong than it was at the beginning when the feared situation provoked considerably more discomfort. In this way, exposure participants learn that if they just "stick it out" and bear the initial discomfort, they will eventually feel better even without doing a ritual.

Imagined Exposure

As in systematic desensitization, exposure to obsessive fears can be given either in imagination or in reality. Is one method better than the other? Researchers have found that, in general, actual exposure *(in vivo)* to feared situations is more effective than fantasy exposure. This seems logical since the first is so much more direct. Touching the door handle to a public restroom stall will be a more powerful experience than imagining touching it.

But there are some situations in which direct exposure is difficult to accomplish in therapy. For example, a person who fears making a major error at work and getting fired for it will have a difficult time constructing this feared scenario in therapy. But he could *imagine* it with great accuracy. After all, most of his obsessive discomfort is due to imagined threats to his job, such as forgetting to do an important task or losing vital papers. He would readily agree that his checking is excessive, and that it in fact impairs his job performance more than any of the mistakes he fears. His imagination of catastrophe is the real source of the difficulty. In this kind of situation, patients seem to benefit more from a *combination* of imagined exposure and actual exposure (for example, deliberately making inconsequential errors). Direct exposure alone doesn't seem to be sufficient to prevent a relapse of the checking and repeating rituals common to such situations. Thus, when the person's obsessive fears are mainly focused on preventing potential disasters, imagined exposure to these ideas can be quite helpful. This type of treatment will be discussed further in Chapter 7.

Speed of Exposure

Should exposure progress gradually, beginning with situations that provoke only very mild anxiety, or should it jump directly to very upsetting situations? Common sense might suggest the first. And, indeed, desensitization uses a very gradual strategy. But as we described earlier, this method has not worked well for obsessive fears. In fact, research shows that if you start at the top of the hierarchy, exposure treatment will be just as effective as if you start midway. Still, starting at the top places tremendous initial strain on people with OCD; they're more likely to quit before they begin. Most clinicians have adopted a method of presenting *moderately* difficult situations first: items that are about a third to half-way up a scale of difficulty. Then increasingly difficult problem areas are worked on as the lower level ones become easier. This method will be used in the treatment guidelines outlined in this book.

The Therapist's Role in Exposure

A final and important concern about the exposure treatment process is whether a therapist needs to be present for treatment to be effective. One researcher compared the effects of therapist-conducted treatment with self-controlled exposure (involving very minimal therapist involvement), and found them to be approximately equally effective. In fact, on average the therapist-treated patients required *more* sessions over time than did the self-controlled ones. It seems as if those who took control of their own exposure treatment learned how to manage their fears more effectively. They also have a better chance of maintaining their improvement in the months and years following treatment. These results have important implications for the usefulness of a self-help book such as this. Some people with OCD will undoubtedly want regular discussion with a professional mental health-care provider, both for support in dealing with the complicated and upsetting symptoms of the disorder, and for help in planning and implementing an exposure treatment program. Others whose symptoms are less severe will need to rely less on professional aid. This is particularly true once sufferers understand the principles behind the treatment and how best to plan and carry out their own exposure and response prevention. Those who prefer self-help are likely to see their fears as largely groundless and to feel highly motivated to resolve their problems. The program isn't easy—self-help readers will need to be able to tolerate a substantial amount of discomfort and fear on their own. The discomfort is an inevitable early by-product of ritualless exposure treatment, with or without professional counseling. In any setting, these feelings will subside. What the self-help reader gives up in support, he or she gains in control and what seem to be faster, more lasting results.

Variants of Response Prevention

When compulsive behaviors or actions are "prevented" during treatment, they are *voluntarily* given up by the patient. No one, including the therapist, actually physically *restrains* the patient from washing or checking. The obsessive-compulsive person must decide for him- or herself not to carry out the rituals. Of course, the therapist strongly urges him or her to avoid doing compulsive actions. Often the therapist is available by phone for emergency situations to help talk the patient out of strong urges to give in to compulsions.

Relatively little attention has been given to variations in the manner of ritual prevention. The only studied aspect of this process is the degree of strictness used in stopping rituals, and even this has been studied only indirectly. A very strict form of response prevention was used by Meyer's staff. They turned off all the faucets in the hospital rooms of patients who performed washing rituals. Nurses or attendants accompanied patients to the bathroom at all times to monitor use of water. No showers or handwashing were permitted except as essential for hygienic reasons. Other programs in England as well as elsewhere (for example, Holland) have been considerably more lenient, allowing a daily 10-minute shower and handwashing in circumstances where non-obsessive people would ordinarily wash, such as after using the bathroom or before cooking or eating. Midway between Meyer's strictness and the less restrictive English programs are some in the United States, where patients may shower once every three to five days but are asked to avoid all handwashing. This type of program has led to substantial improvement in 75 to 80 percent of the patients.

A considerably less restrictive form of response prevention has been labelled "response delay." In this method, a waiting period is required between the occurrence of obsessive thoughts and the compulsive checking, cleaning, or other ritual. The waiting period may be gradually increased from several minutes to several hours. This response delay procedure has been found effective in two reported cases, but has not been tried on a large scale with many patients.

Although the response prevention programs described above have never been directly compared, it appears that the *best results* are produced for people with OCD who follow *strict regimens*. Avoiding washing as much as possible and eliminating all but essential one-time checking of important circumstances seems to be the best strategy for reducing washing and checking compulsions. For those with rituals of repeating certain actions or placing things in a certain order, these rituals must be stopped altogether. Chapter 9 will discuss plans for restricting your own ritualistic actions.

Are Both Exposure and Response Prevention Necessary?

This chapter has outlined various forms of exposure treatments and response prevention strategies. Meyer, as well as other researchers around the world, tried applying both procedures simultaneously. Investigators in Philadelphia sought to determine whether both were essential and why. They compared exposure alone without any restriction on rituals, response prevention alone, and the combination of the two. Their findings from two studies clearly indicated that the combined treatment program worked best. Obsessive fears, they discovered, diminished considerably after prolonged exposure treatment. The fears did not decrease after simple response prevention (blocking rituals without introducing the feared situation). Just the reverse was true for compulsive rituals; these diminished most when they were blocked with response prevention strategies, but improved very little when exposure was used by itself. Therefore, to best reduce both types of symptoms, both exposure and restriction of compulsions are necessary.

Summary

Researchers have slowly pieced together a picture of the optimal therapeutic approach to OCD. A successful treatment is one that addresses both the obsessive fears and the compulsive rituals of OCD, diminishing both. Systematic desensitization was *not* found to be helpful to most OCD sufferers, either in alleviating obsessive fears significantly or in diminishing the need to ritualize. But lengthy exposure to feared situations has proven quite successful in reducing obsessive fears.

Exposure to an obsessive situation should last for more than a few minutes, perhaps for hours. It's sometimes helpful to have someone demonstrate the feared action first. For those whose fears center around catastrophes, imagined exposure to the circumstances surrounding those "disasters" appears to be quite helpful. Whether delivered imaginally or in reality, exposure should begin with moderately disturbing situations and progress gradually toward more difficult ones. The presence of a therapist may be necessary in some cases, but many people with Obsessive Compulsive Disorder are able to carry out exposure on their own without continuous help from a trained professional

Lengthy exposure by itself addresses only half the problem. With respect to treatment of compulsions, strict elimination of rituals during exposure appears to be the best strategy. A few good results have been achieved in studies with less strict methods, but most OCD patients improve best by learning that their fears can diminish without any resort to ritual. We should note that there are a few people who are so successful in avoiding their feared situations that they practice few, if any, rituals. Some do this by completely staying away from obsessive circumstances (for example, not going outside to avoid checking for stones or nails that might harm others). Others use drugs or alcohol to drown anxiety responses so that rituals are less necessary to accomplish this end. Needless to say, both strategies produce further complications.

Overall, the outlook for those suffering from Obsessive Compulsive Disorder is quite positive. About two-thirds to three-fourths of the patients in therapy programs that include exposure and response prevention have shown substantial and lasting improvements. This is particularly true for those who are highly motivated to improve, and willing to tolerate the discomfort of exposing themselves to fearful situations and controlling their urges to ritualize.

In the next several chapters, we will provide step-by-step strategies for 1) reducing obsessive fears by imaginal and actual exposure and 2) eliminating compulsive rituals through response prevention. The chapters are designed to be read through completely before beginning, and then re-read slowly while putting the relevant parts into practice. These instructions and exercises may be used alone without the aid of a professional therapist (psychologist, social worker, psychiatrist, psychiatric nurse, etc.), or they may be use in the context of professional help at the direction of the therapist. Since these methods have been carefully researched with hundreds of patients, it is very likely that you will find them of considerable benefit in reducing your own obsessive-compulsive problems.

6

Reducing Obsessions and Compulsions: The Planning Stage

Getting Up the Courage

It requires a great deal of motivation and courage for a person with Obsessive Compulsive Disorder (OCD) to begin an exposure treatment program. After all, the treatment is based on confronting one's obsessive fears and preventing the compulsive acts that ease those fears. Researchers in behavioral treatment for OCD have noted that as many as 25 to 30 percent of those who consider entering such psychological treatment programs decide not to attempt it. In many cases, these people seek medication treatment despite the fact that behavioral treatment has been shown to be quite effective with OCD and possibly more helpful than drug therapy (refer to Chapter 10 for more detail on this issue).

Their reluctance is understandable, if unfortunate. Behavioral treatment involves deciding to expose oneself to the very situations that gave rise to so much avoidance and compulsive effort to neutralize the fear. It is perhaps akin to a height phobic person electing to go up in a hot air balloon or a speech phobic agreeing to give a talk to 200 people. Neither of these actions is actually dangerous, but it can feel terrifying at the time. Of course, exposure treatment is nearly always done in a gradual fashion. Nonetheless, the experience of fear is an inevitable part of the exposure treatment process.

How do you muster the courage to begin? There is no simple answer. For most obsessive-compulsives, it is a matter of weighing the discomfort of treatment against the burden of their daily struggle with obsessions and rituals. Most OCD sufferers find themselves anxious, depressed, and frustrated at their limited functioning before undertaking treatment. Particularly if the OCD symptoms have lasted for some years and/or have not responded adequately to medication, exposure treatment usually proves easier in the long run than living with such restricting and upsetting symptoms. Mustering the courage to begin confronting those fears is never easy. But regular reminders of the potential benefits and the very probability that you *will* benefit from exposure may help you keep your goals in mind.

Do You Need Professional Help?

The decision to seek professional help from a behaviorally trained therapist rests on several factors. People with very severe obsessive and compulsive symptoms—fears and rituals that consume many hours per day—are likely to require professional help, since the problem can seem too overwhelming to face alone. Professional therapy may also be needed when OCD symptoms are very complex and therefore difficult for the person to describe or record on paper. Especially when cognitive compulsions alternate in close association with obsessive ideas, an experienced therapist may offer crucial help in determining when to apply exposure and when to block or avoid the obsessive thoughts. Finally, some people feel more motivated and work harder and more consistently toward their goals when they have to report to another person or group of people. If you are the sort of person who prefers to diet or give up a bad habit by joining a support group or teaming up with a friend, then regular contact with a therapist may be a good strategy for achieving your aims.

Once you decide you need professional help, how do you select a therapist? Although many mental health professionals believe they can treat OCD, many are inadequately trained or experienced in the specific treatment of this disorder. The person you choose for treatment should have both 1) *direct experience* in applying exposure and response prevention with several cases of OCD (or be immediately supervised by a professional with such experience) and 2) *behavioral training* in this method from another professional experienced in treatment of OCD (preferably, though not necessarily, someone who has published professional papers in this area).

Do not hesitate to ask a prospective therapist questions about his or her training (what type and by whom) and experience, including how many people with OCD he or she has treated and what the results have been. A good therapist will not resent the questions, but rather assume that you are appropriately concerned about obtaining high quality treatment for your problem.

To obtain the names of prospective therapists in your area, you can contact the OCD Foundation at P.O. Box 9573, New Haven, CT 06535. Their referrals may include behavior therapists as well as physicians expert in the *drug* treatment of OCD, but not in behavior therapy. Or you may contact the Association for the Advancement of Behavior Therapy (AABT) at 15 West 36th St., New York, NY 10018 for a listing of their behaviorally trained members (usually these are psychologists). Members of the latter organization will have training in behavior therapy, but may not be trained or experienced in the treatment of OCD. You will have to investigate this for yourself.

Another strategy is to contact people who have published research papers in this area: often they can refer you to someone nearby who is well-trained, perhaps even someone they have trained themselves. Again, bear in mind the distinction between pharmacotherapists (psychiatrists expert in prescribing drugs for OCD) and behavior therapists; both may have something valuable to offer you, but they won't be the same things. A pharmacotherapist with experience in OCD may also be able to refer you to a good behavior therapist.

Of course, once you locate a suitable therapist, you'll want to be sure you feel comfortable with this person and able to work well together. Therapy should be a positive learning experience for you. You should feel that your therapist asks helpful questions in trying to clarify the nature of your difficulties. You'll want to be given useful information about the nature of your OCD symptoms and about the treatment plan. A good therapist will be supportive and encouraging, but very firm in urging you to expose yourself to fearful situations and to stop your rituals.

Remember, however, that your must carry out the therapy instructions yourself, to the best of your ability. The more involved the OCD sufferer is in his or her treatment, the more effective treatment is likely to be, especially over the long term. It is important that *you* learn and understand the treatment methods. Even with the therapist's guidance you'll need to take much of the initiative yourself.

The key, then, to successful professional treatment involves a balanced combination of factors: a therapist with adequate behavioral training, specific experience in treating OCD, and a manner that you feel comfortable with, as well as your own motivation and commitment to the process. Keep in mind that in behavior therapy of OCD, the technique may be as important as the personality and manner of the therapist. A very likeable and sympathetic therapist who does not employ the right techniques may be quite unable to help you, but may be hard for you to give up. You may wish to keep periodic contact with a therapist who has been treating you for other problems, while you see a behavior therapist for your OCD symptoms. It is important that the two therapists consult with each other at the beginning of such an arrangement so you do not receive conflicting suggestions during treatment.

The remainder of this chapter is designed for those who wish to try to control their OCD symptoms without professional help or who are using this book at their therapist's suggestion as an aid to professional treatment.

Before You Start

Before you can begin to plan a treatment program for yourself, you must first define your OCD symptoms very clearly. You need to figure out what your own obsessions consist of and what specific compulsive thoughts or actions you have been using to relieve your obsessive fears. Unless you are quite thorough about this process, you are likely to plan an inadequate program. This might only partly meet your needs, and would put you at high risk for failure or relapse. Remember that this is possibly the most important part of your treatment program. We recommend that you carefully follow each of the steps described below.

You might find it helpful to read through this whole chapter—and the two that follow if you wish—before beginning your treatment program. That way you'll know what's ahead, and why each step is an important part of the program. Or you may wish to begin right away, making notes as they occur to you and gradually adding on to them.

Defining Your Compulsions

It will be easiest to begin with your compulsive actions and work backward to compulsive thoughts and then to your obsessions. Remember that in the first chapters, compulsions were defined as thoughts and actions a person engages in to relieve anxiety, fear, or some other unpleasant emotion like disgust or guilt. Start by listing each general type of behavior or action that you have been doing in a repetitive or stereotypic way (see Chart 1 at the end of this chapter). These are actions that you feel you have little choice about doing—you are compelled by discomfort and force of habit. If you didn't do them, you would feel tension, fear, etc. In addition, you feel pretty sure that the behavior is really unnecessary. Or, at least, you believe it isn't necessary to do as often or as carefully as you do.

Consider the following typical examples, as mentioned earlier:

- washing your hands or other parts of your body because they don't feel "clean"
- washing or cleaning other things or possibly people (your children) or pets to get them "clean"
- checking to verify that something has been done by you or by others (for example, checking that the door is locked, checking that the iron is off)
- checking to verify that something inappropriate or wrongful has not been done by you or by others (for example, forgetting something, throwing out important papers)
- repeating an action (often in a particular order or specific way or a certain number of times) to "magical-

ly" or "superstitiously" prevent some catastrophe you
are worried about
- repeating particular words, phrases, or sentences
- placing objects in a particular order or configuration
- saving things you are afraid you might need someday
- requesting reassurance from others around you that
  something has been done or said properly

There are, of course, other behaviors or thoughts you
might have that meet the qualifications for compulsions.
Include these in your list, even if you are not certain whether
they are truly compulsions. In this case, it is better to err on
the side of including too much. You can always decide later
that some behavior is not really a problem or that it is a
different sort of problem and not part of the OCD symptoms.
If you have any confusion at this point about what qualifies
as a compulsion or ritual, go back to Chapter 2 for a reminder.

Remember that some thoughts or mental events can be
just as ritualistic as behaviors. For example, if you silently say
a particular prayer over and over until you feel better, this is
probably more than just following the teachings of your
religion. Write it down on the list. You might count things in
your head. Other cognitive or mental compulsions include
forming a particular mental image with all of the "right"
details until you feel relieved. You might repeat certain
phrases in your mind or continually "start over" until you
feel you have the proper "mind set" to do a task correctly.
Perhaps you make mental lists in an extremely careful way,
so as not to forget something. Mental or cognitive rituals, as
they are often called, can be difficult to identify, since they
happen inside your head where no one can see the repetitive,
stereotypic, or compulsive quality they have. Notice that
they have the same feeling attached to them as overt compulsions do, especially if you were to try *not* to engage in them:

you would feel you could not stop, that you must do it or you would have no peace of mind.

Of course, everyone has habits, and most people would feel some mild discomfort if they did them differently or gave them up altogether. For example, you might keep your pens in certain places where you feel they "belong" or arrange the knickknacks in your house in a particular order that pleases you. If this were a ritual, you would be unable to change the location without a considerable amount of discomfort and reluctance. You might also feel that something bad would happen if you did. If it were merely a habit or an organizational preference, you could much more easily change at least the location of the objects, especially if someone you respected gave a rational reason for the advantage to the change. The key aspect of the rituals that you need to record is that they relieve discomfort and would be very difficult for you to give up or change.

After you have listed basic rituals, you'll need to make a more detailed list. For example, if you wash yourself in a compulsive way, describe your pattern of washing. Do you wash in a special order or in a particular manner? Must you start or end your shower with a certain body part so as not to "contaminate" other parts? When you wash your hands, do you have to do so in a particular bathroom or in a special way? For example, you might use paper towels to touch the faucets, or wash them first so they seem "clean" when you turn them off with your newly cleaned hands. Perhaps you wash each finger individually, or wash up to the elbow, or count to six for each part, or wash four times rather than once.

If one of your rituals is checking, note whether you have to do this in a particular order or a certain number of times. Maybe you have to stare at something to convince yourself you are really seeing it. You may have to repeat some phrase to yourself to confirm that you have "properly" checked something. Usually, how long or how often you check or repeat an action depends on your degree of discomfort—the more tension or guilt or other unpleasant emotion you feel, the more you must do the ritual until you feel relieved.

To be sure you have all of the details you need in your list of rituals, keep a diary for at least three days, and preferably for a week (see Chart 2 at the end of this chapter). This will give you a very accurate picture of how and when you do your compulsions. Keeping this list may not be easy. You may feel embarrassed just to think about your symptoms. Just assure yourself that your list is private, and intended only for your own benefit.

Before you begin, read the section below on obsessions so you can record both obsessions and compulsions at once. You can use the charts at the end of this chapter for this purpose or create your own to suit your needs. While you are recording your rituals, try not to change your behavior just because you are observing it carefully. Most people find that they have a tendency to reduce their rituals when recording because it is so unpleasant to see how compulsively they behave. Resist this urge. You will be working on reducing compulsions soon enough. For now, just get a realistic picture of your habitual actions and mental patterns.

Defining Your Obsessions

The easiest way to identify your obsessions is to take note of the situations that lead to your compulsions. If obsessions increase discomfort and compulsions reduce it, then prior to each compulsive act or thought, there should be some event or idea or situation that increases your tension level and leads you to feel compelled to ritualize.

As discussed earlier, there are two aspects to your obsessions which you will need to define. The first is the concrete or tangible source of obsessive fear. This is the actual object or situation, or the mental ideas, images, or impulses that trigger immediate fear (record in column 3 of your diary—see Chart 2). You will find that these are situations you try to *avoid* as best you can. The second aspect to an obsession is the disaster or catastrophe that you are afraid would occur if you did not do your ritual (record in column 4 of your diary). Not all OCD sufferers have fears of disastrous consequences. For example, not everyone who washes excessively because of bathroom "germs" believes that they might get a disease; some merely feel "dirty" or disgusted without concern for possible harm. It is important for you to question yourself about your fears of future consequences. You will eventually need to incorporate these fears, if they exist, into your treatment program.

The performance of a ritual is your cue to look for a source of obsessive fear. You can trace your immediate action and thoughts backwards to pinpoint the two components of an obsession: the tangible source of fear and the feared consequences. Recording each ritual you perform in your diary will help focus your attention on each source of fear in your day.

Tangible Sources of Obsessive Fear. If you have washing or cleaning rituals, chances are that each time you wash, you feel concerned about some type of "contamination," "dirt," or "uncleanness." The source of this sense of contamination varies widely from person to person. Your concern might stem from bathroom "germs" that lead you to avoid faucets, toilet seats, trash cans, etc. Human bodily secretions like sweat, mucus, urine, feces, and blood are often the source of avoidance of restrooms or other public places. Lately, AIDS has become an especially common fear. Other common sources of washing compulsions include pesticides or other chemical substances, sources of radiation, animals, or certain people (for example, homosexuals, one's parents). Many individuals with OCD have highly idiosyncratic sources of fear and contamination. We have seen people concerned about touching objects from New York City, or a grave site, or chocolate. In such cases, the feared and avoided situation usually represents an earlier event or relationship that was very upsetting or led to considerable conflict. If you have obsessive fears that seem unusual, rest assured that these are equally likely to respond well to the treatment methods outlined in this book.

For those who have checking rituals, the tangible sources of obsessive fear or guilt are often circumstances such as leaving the house for the day or getting out of the car. These actions may provoke fears that lights will be left on, faucets running, objects too close to sources of fire (furnace, stove, heater), electrical appliances running or plugged in, etc. Other sources of anxiety might be driving in the car (for fear of hitting a pedestrian), throwing out empty bags or envelopes (for fear of discarding important papers), or walking down the sidewalk and seeing trash (which might be notes you had written) or broken glass (which might hurt someone if you don't pick it up). For those with checking rituals, the specific concrete situations seem less important than the imagined potential consequences of failing to check. This is discussed further below.

Tangible sources of fear for persons with repeating rituals are often more difficult to identify. Sometimes they're not even a relevant factor in the obsessive fears. A woman who repeats her dressing routine three times in an exact order because she thinks it might prevent her husband from having an auto accident on his way home from work is responding to internal thoughts or ideas, rather than to external, concrete situations. Often, the repeated actions are those that happen at the time the fearful thoughts appear. For example, if you think of your mother dying while you are stepping off the sidewalk into the street, you may feel obliged to back up and step down again without the "bad thought."

In other cases, however, certain situations do spark the urge to repeat an action. One woman felt compelled to repeat the words on every street sign she passed, although she was not at all sure what she thought would happen if she failed to do this. In her case, street signs were a concrete cue for rituals. Another man repeated a particular prayer in a precise manner whenever he cut in front of someone on the highway or drove in a seemingly "reckless" way that might endanger another driver. Some OCD sufferers repeatedly retrace their driving routes to be sure that they did not hit a pedestrian inadvertently. These people tend to become especially uncomfortable along busy city routes where pedestrians abound, or on streets with potholes where they might mistake a big bump for the experience of running over a pedestrian.

Feared Disastrous Consequences. As mentioned above, those with obsessions about "dirt" or "contamination" will usually but not always have a clear idea of why they fear a particular situation. They may fear catastrophes such as getting leukemia, cancer, herpes, AIDS, or some other serious disease. Or they may be fearful of giving this disease to someone else, usually someone very close to them like a child or a spouse. In some cases, they may fear causing harm to complete strangers. If you have washing rituals, ask yourself what serious consequence you fear might happen if you refused to wash your hands the next time you felt compelled to do so.

Note that in some cases of washing and cleaning rituals, individuals cannot identify any particular disease or harmful consequence that they fear. They may merely feel that the anxiety would be too much for them to manage; that the anxiety would never decrease or would lead them to "go crazy." Or they may feel unsure about what the consequence would be exactly, just that something very bad would happen. This can be described as a sense of doom or foreboding.

It is relatively rare to find that someone with checking rituals has no fear of disastrous consequences if he or she doesn't check. As psychologist Jack Rachman has pointed out, checking rituals are generally performed to *prevent* harm from happening to oneself or to others. The feared harm is usually apparent in the nature of the checking ritual itself. Checks of door locks are often attempts to prevent burglars from gaining entry into the house; checks of empty envelopes prevent the loss of important papers; picking up glass shards on the sidewalk prevent others from hurting themselves; checking the rear view mirror avoids unwittingly leaving run-over pedestrians behind on the highway. Although the feared consequence is often logically related to the situation that provokes the fear and to the type of ritual, this does not mean that it is reasonable.

It is doubtful that you would be reading this book if you did not feel that your fear and ritualistic behavior were excessive or inappropriate to the circumstances that provoke them. Chances are that your fears about failing to check "properly" are considerably overblown, certainly more than people around you experience. In your mind, you have probably either distorted the probability of the consequences you fear or exaggerated the amount of harm that would ensue. Perhaps you would just "rather be safe than sorry." This applies to fears of disastrous consequences for those with washing and checking rituals, as well as certain other types. See Chapter 13 for additional discussion of the patterns of thinking that often accompany obsessive fears.

Like checking rituals, repeating rituals are usually carried out to prevent possible harm to oneself or others. Unlike them, however, the action that is repeated is often not at all logically connected with the feared disaster. For example, dressing and undressing in a stereotypic fashion has no logical connection with one's husband's driving experience;

it could only prevent an accident in a magical sort of way. Stepping forward or backward across a threshold or through a doorway does not logically undo a "bad" thought about harm to one's mother. There is a superstitious quality that links the ritual to the feared consequence.

It may be apparent from the preceding discussion that obsessive feared consequences follow a common pattern. They are usually exaggerated versions of normal fears most people have. Obsessive fears tend to focus on disease, death, harming or killing others, or being responsible (guilty) for mistakes that provoke criticism or rejection from others. Occasionally, people with OCD hold to strong beliefs that their feared consequences are actually likely to occur. That is, they are not really convinced of the senselessness of their obsessions and compulsions. In such cases, it is best to explore the logic behind the fear first to see if the belief can be altered before attempting any exposure and prevention of rituals. This does not refer to those who, when suddenly faced with a highly fearful obsessive circumstance, begin to believe in the need to do the ritual. People with OCD often become confused about the reasonableness of their fears when they are highly agitated. Rather, it is the person who firmly believes that his or her fears are realistic even when he or she is calm. In such cases, additional talk therapy prior to exposure is advised.

Record Keeping

Keeping a careful record of your symptoms is an extremely important part of planning a successful behavioral treatment program. It is also very difficult, since the record is an all too real reminder of the very symptoms you would probably least like to pay close attention to.

Your daily diary should include careful noting of all your rituals, including concrete sources of fear behind them. Try to notice whenever you are avoiding doing something that others appear to do readily. This record will help you generate the list of situations you'll eventually use for exposure treatment (Chart 3). A format you might use for your diary is given at the end of this chapter (Chart 2). Even if you create your own system, be sure to allow room for listing the triggers of the obsessive fears, as well as feared consequences that are related to them.

Once you are satisfied that your daily diary contains a complete, accurate record of your rituals and fears over several days, it's time to create a more condensed list. This final list will focus on your obsessions. By combining columns 3 and 4 from your diary of rituals, you can identify your specific obsessions. For instance, if you noted that you washed your hands for five minutes around 3:00, you'll know that an obsession was brought to mind then. From column 3, you might see that the trigger of the ritual was leaving a public restroom. From column 4, you might recall that the specific consequence you feared was coming into contact with a disease-causing germ, and dying. The general obsession these entries point to is a fear of touching the doorknob in a public restroom. That would be an entry in your list of obsessions (Chart 3).

Try to consider all sources of obsessive fear from your daily diary, as well as from memory of other situations that led to rituals in the past. Don't worry if you find that your list of obsessions is quite lengthy, or that some listings are more significant than others. Once your list is complete, you'll rank the specific situations in order of degree of difficulty (degree of anxiety or discomfort generated). Chapter 7 will discuss how to do this. All this—from observing and diary keeping to list creating—is geared to help you decide what to include in your exposure treatment.

In trying to clarify your fears, ask yourself whether you have fears of disastrous consequences that fall into any of the general areas described above: disease, for instance, or accidental death of a loved one, etc. Then specify more precisely what exactly you are afraid might happen if you did not do your ritual.

In addition to your daily diary and your condensed list of obsessive fears and rituals, you may wish to write a brief history of the onset and development of your symptoms. Such a history can help remind you of situations that still provoke discomfort, even though you may rarely encounter them. Include these situations in your list of fear-provoking situations.

Summary

The first step in planning a successful treatment program is making a firm decision to conquer your obsessive fears and ritualistic behaviors. This can be a hard step to take. A professional therapist trained in behavioral treatment might prove helpful to you, depending upon the complexity, severity, and pervasiveness of your fears and rituals. Suggestions for locating and evaluating a therapist's qualifications are noted earlier in this chapter. Whether you work alone or with a therapist, you'll need to concentrate on identifying your compulsive behaviors or thoughts. To do this you need to keep a careful record of the actual behaviors, their frequency or duration, and any specific thoughts or fears that accompany them. If you also note *when* your compulsions occur, it will be easier for you to recognize the types of situations that lead to the compulsions and the specific obsessive fears behind the compulsive behavior. If you find yourself believing that your feared disasters really are likely to occur, you will need to address the logic of these beliefs before undertaking exposure and ritual prevention treatment. Record keeping throughout the process of treatment is a very important part of effective therapy.

Chart 1

List of Rituals

Begin by listing each general behavior or action that you have been doing in a repetitive way (i.e., washing, cleaning, checking, repeating, counting, hoarding, requesting reassurance, etc.). Then go back over your list, adding as much detail as you can. You may come back to this list to add more detail after keeping a daily diary for several days (see Chart 2).

Type of Ritual	Specific Action
ex. Repeating	*Stepping back to where a bad thought occurred, fixing the thought, and stepping forward again with the positive thought.*

1.

2.

3.

4.

5.

6.

7.

8.

9.

10.

Chart 2

Daily Diary of Rituals

Date_____

Compulsive rituals performed (list here, and assign letters for use below:
for example, A=washing, B=checking, C=asking for reassurance, etc.):

A_____
B_____
C_____
D_____
E_____

Hour	Type of Ritual (use letters from above)	Minutes Spent on Ritual	Trigger of Ritual (object, event, or idea)	Specific Fear or Feared Consequence
6 a.m.				
7 a.m.				
8 a.m.				
9 a.m.				
10 a.m.				
11 a.m.				
12 noon				
1 p.m.				
2 p.m.				
3 p.m.				
4 p.m.				
5 p.m.				
6 p.m.				
7 p.m.				
8 p.m.				
9 p.m.				
10 p.m.				
11 p.m.				
12 a.m.				
1 a.m.				
2 a.m.				
3 a.m.				
4 a.m.				
5 a.m.				

Chart 3
List of Obsessive Thoughts and Images

This list of obsessions will form the basis of your exposure program. Use the information from your daily diary (Chart 2) to make this list as complete and specific as possible. Refer to columns 3 and 4 of the diary— what triggered a ritual, and what disastrous consequence you feared—to identify the specific obsession behind each of your rituals. For further instructions on describing your discomfort level, refer to Chapter 7.

Obsessions or Obsessive Situations	Discomfort Level (0-100)
ex: *Touching the doorknob in a public restroom*	*40*
Touching the toilet seat in a public restroom	*70*

1.

2.

3.

4.

5.

6.

7.

8.

9.

10.

7

Reducing Obsessive Fears: Direct Exposure

Note: Be sure to read Chapters 7-9 before beginning treatment.

This chapter is designed to help people with obsessive fears plan and carry out a treatment program tailored to their own specific needs. If you plan to embark on such a program, it is essential that you first complete a list of feared obsessive situations, as described in the previous chapter. The situations on your list should be those that cause you to feel uncomfortable (anxious, nervous, guilty, etc.), that you work to avoid, or that provoke your rituals. It is best if you keep a record for at least three days and preferably for a week of all of the situations you encounter that actually lead to compulsive behavior or thoughts. The previous chapter should help you organize your record-keeping and list-making; those written records will form the basis for the exposure treatment plan you'll develop in this chapter.

Recall from Chapter 5 that the best available psychological treatment for "Obsessive Compulsive Disorder" (OCD) is exposure and ritual prevention. In this method, people with OCD are asked to confront their feared obsessive situations (either directly or through visualization), *and at the same time* severely restrict or eliminate their rituals. This therapy has resulted in considerable improvement for most of the patients who have received it. Many experienced a great reduction in obsessive fears and urges to ritualize; rituals decreased to very low frequency. Some patients were considered nearly recovered; only a minority failed to hold on to gains made. No one was worse for the effort. These positive results come from studies in which exposure was directed by a therapist who planned the treatment program with the patient's help. The patient him- or herself was always responsible for the actual execution of the exposure, even when it was done with the therapist's direction during therapy sessions. In addition, patients were almost always given homework assignments to carry out on their own or with the help of family members or close friends.

You may remember that in one study, patients who carried out their own exposure treatment with minimal help from a therapist did as well as those who had regular therapy sessions. The self-help patients benefited a great deal from the therapy, and their gains proved particularly lasting. Planning and executing your own exposure therapy, then, is likely to be rewarding: chances are that you can reduce your obsessions and compulsions on a permanent basis.

Keep in mind, however, that this is not an easy program. You will need all your courage and patience to carry it out. You will probably also need the help of a close friend or relative. This chapter provides the necessary guidelines for planning and carrying out direct exposure to your feared situations. The real work, of course, remains with you (as would be true in any treatment program). You should not begin direct exposure without also beginning to limit your rituals, although at first the temptation to ritualize will be strong. For that reason you'll need to read through Chapter 9 before beginning. Chapter 8 describes imagined exposure techniques, which you may wish to try. Be sure to read all three chapters first, and then come back to the beginning of this chapter so you can proceed in the most effective way possible.

Making a Hierarchy

Look at the list of fear-provoking situations and objects that you've been working on. It's time to rank each item on this list according to how uncomfortable (fearful, guilty, nervous) it causes you to feel. For this purpose, behavior therapists usually use a scale of 0 to 100 in which 0 represents no discomfort at all and 100 is the most uncomfortable (frightened, panicky) you have ever felt in your life. To become familiar with this scale, think now of times in your life when you were completely relaxed, that is, at 0. Remember how you felt physically and mentally then, so that you can compare your current feeling state with that zero point. Perhaps it was reading in the shade last summer; perhaps it was curled up watching a fire on a winter night with your pet sleeping beside you. Try to recall your physical comfort then, your general peace of mind, and your freedom from distractibility. Now think of a time when you were at 100: the most uncomfortable you have *ever* felt, a time when you confronted your fear head-on. Remember how you felt then physically and psychologically: perhaps your heart beat fast or you were sweating, your muscles tensed up, your knees went weak, or your head felt dizzy. What were your immediate thoughts then? To run? Freeze? Try to recall every physical detail so that when you use this scale, you can compare your feelings in different situations. You want to learn to rate each situation on your own scale of 0 to 100.

For example, how would you rate yourself at this very moment? As you wonder what number to assign to your feelings, what thoughts or sensations are you aware of? Do you have a tell-tale response to slight fear (sweaty palms, unclear thoughts) that you feel now? Remember that the scale is personal—you decide what 30 or 75 feels like. All you are trying to do is learn how to compare one obsessive situation with another, in order to rank them according to how uncomfortable and difficult they are for you.

Once you have a feeling for how to use the scale, put a number from 0 to 100 after each situation that you fear or avoid or that causes you to ritualize. When you're done, write out a new list, ordering the situations from lowest to highest difficulty. You might find it helpful to draw up separate lists for each particular obsessive fear: perhaps the diary you kept can help you break them down by type. (Examples will be given later in this chapter.) The result will be your *hierarchy* (or hierarchies) of obsessive feared situations. It will be the basis of your exposure treatment.

At this point, many people find that the situations they have listed are not specific enough to be rated easily. You may find yourself saying, "It depends on the circumstance." This probably means that you have not been quite specific enough about the factors or variables that make some situations worse than others. Now is the time to clarify exactly what situations or objects trigger your obsessive thoughts and compulsive rituals. The sample lists below—already ranked by patients in order of obsessive fear—may help you work out how your own hierarchy will look. Keep in mind that these are brief lists for the sake of example and that yours is likely to be much longer.

One part-time nurse feared that slivers of glass would become lodged in clothing or household objects. She particularly worried that her young daughter, Katrina, or her husband would touch or swallow the slivers and become seriously ill or die. To relieve her fears, she repeatedly washed, brushed, or wiped herself, the family clothing, and places where she thought she might have seen glass. Her hands were raw from constant use of soap and water. She also had three other types of obsessive fears that were successfully treated, but this one was the most problematic. Her hierarchy for this obsessive problem was as follows:

Situation	Anxiety
playing with Katrina on kitchen floor	40
using money from pocket	40
putting certain shirt on Katrina	45
using deodorant from cabinet	45
wearing certain slacks	50
using a certain tablecloth	55
changing kitchen curtains	55
putting flowers in glass vase	60
bringing Katrina's toys inside	65
changing Katrina's diaper without washing	70
cleaning out storage closet	80
using entire desk where pictures were	85
letting Katrina roam freely in her bedroom	85
sitting on living room chairs	90
putting Katrina's toys on her bed	90
allowing Katrina to roam freely in house	95
putting pictures in glass frames	95
cleaning broken glass in kitchen	99
cleaning broken glass on boat	100

As you might imagine, all of the above situations in some way involved glass that had or might possibly have broken. She was often not sure if there had actually been broken glass in these situations, but felt she would "rather be safe than sorry." This is a common theme for people with OCD, who fear taking even tiny risks when it comes to obsessively feared situations. The above hierarchy represents only about one-third of the actual situations to which this patient was exposed during behavior therapy, but all of them followed the same theme of situations in which slivers of glass might have been overlooked.

Another woman, a university professor, worried obsessively about mistakes she might make that would cause others serious or lasting harm. The types of situations that triggered these feelings varied widely, but all were connected by this theme of potential damage to others that she might have prevented. In particular, she feared giving students grades that did not really reflect their ability relative to others in class, and she feared driving over someone on the highway when she wasn't paying close attention. These situations were followed by extensive mental checking (reviewing what she had done), and actual checking to verify that no mistake had been made. She constructed the following hierarchies (notice how she organized her fears by obsessive situation):

Situation: Being unfair	Anxiety
Giving a student partial credit for an exam question	20
Making up a quiz	40
Grading a quiz	45
Making up a midterm exam	60
Making up the final exam	70
Grading essay exam questions	75
Interviewing for a job elsewhere without telling her current employer	80

Situation: Causing harm to others	
Borrowing small objects from others	20
Doing computations, especially for income tax	35
Driving over small bumps on highway	40
Throwing out papers, envelopes, etc.	50
Driving over large bumps on highway	60
Leaving a large stick on the highway	70
Driving at night on unfamiliar roads	85

Driving from snowy street onto plowed one (carrying snow onto plowed street)	90

Situation: Making a bad choice

Selecting the first item in grocery store	40
Ordering quickly from restaurant menu	45
Throwing out extra copies of important papers	50
Throwing out old clothes	55
Deciding on student grade quickly	65

Multiple Fears and Multiple Hierarchies. This series of hierarchies of obsessive fears provides an example of how to organize a collection of multiple worries. If you fear many different types of situations, it is best to try to identify themes along which the feared situations fall together, in varying intensity. Possible categories might be: contamination from chemicals; contamination from AIDS (or other contagious disease); neglectful actions that might harm your child ("being a bad mother"); thinking "bad" thoughts about loved ones; blaspheming God. This way you can pick one *type* of situation to confront first, and see progress more easily during the exposure treatment. This will encourage you to work toward further gains with other obsessive fears and rituals.

When feared obsessive situations are related to each other theoretically, they are like rungs on a ladder. If you cut off the bottom rung, the whole ladder becomes shorter. Similarly, if you reduce your anxiety by exposure to an item low on your hierarchy, the items higher will seem slightly less anxiety-provoking. This won't necessarily happen for *every* item, but in general, the more you expose yourself to items lower on the list, the more manageable the higher ones will seem. You can use this trend to make your initial progress more obvious: concentrate first on several items from one obsessive theme, rather than on one item from three different themes. You'll be encouraged and heartened by the visible strides toward improvement in that one area. Thus, the woman in the second example above might choose to tackle her fear of "being unfair" first. She would work her way up most of that hierarchy before addressing the next category: causing harm to others.

In the first example above, the patient created her hierarchies according to the severity of disastrous consequences she feared would happen if she did not clean or check. This patient feared glass, but she also feared pesticides and other chemicals that might cause harm to her family. In addition, she felt responsible for family members tripping or hurting themselves if she left objects in their way or did not straighten the corner of a rug. She told herself privately that she might have done such things because she really intended to cause them harm (although it was clear she loved her family dearly). It seemed to her that God would punish her if she failed to correct the situation. In this case, she made several lists, distinguished by the source of her fears (glass, chemicals, neglectful acts). Within each list, she ranked situations according to the severity of the disastrous consequence she anticipated. She began her exposure program by working on her fear of glass, since this fear caused her the most discomfort and inconvenience.

Some people with repeating rituals fear that failure to repeat an action (like buttoning a button or retracing steps) will "magically" permit some disaster (like a car accident) to occur. It is very hard to predict in advance just how much anxiety will occur in a particular situation. In this case, the hierarchy (or hierarchies) will be determined by the estimated amount of obsessive fear the person experiences on a given occasion. One woman, for example, feared several different types of images, many of them religious. All were horrific to her to different degrees. She relieved her anxiety by repeating certain prayers and visualizing a "healing light" when she thought of any of them. Later she developed a need to repeat words and names from signs on the highway, list

colors, and repeat nonsense phrases or particular visual geo-
metric patterns. She carried out these mental rituals in
response to specific verbal or visual cues from her environment.

This person determined her list of feared situations by
writing down all the types of images and sounds that might
trigger a ritual and rank-ordering them according to the
degree of anxiety she was likely to experience. The hierarchy
was not always precise, because some days she felt more
uncomfortable in a specific situation than she did on other
days. Still, there was an observable pattern to her obsessive
fears, in that the religious images always provoked more
anxiety than the more neutral signs or phrases or visual cues.
The religious images, then, were on the severe end of the list.

Once you have developed a hierarchy, it is a good idea to
show it to one or two people who know you well and can
comment, in a neutral manner, on whether you left anything
out or whether their own observations support the order in
which you have placed the situations. Of course, you are
always the final judge of how disturbing a situation is to you;
only you can really know. However, they may have noticed
that you avoid certain situations without even realizing it.
The input of observant family members or friends can often
help in this.

Exposure

Beginning Exposure

If your hierarchy seems to revolve heavily around disastrous consequences that are often on your mind, you may
need to include exposure in imagination to these ideas, along
with the direct confrontation we are about to describe. We
suggest that you first plan and begin the direct exposures
before you decide whether imagining the feared consequen-

ces in a more structured way will be needed to reduce your obsessive fears. Of course, in some cases direct exposure is not really possible because of the nature of the obsessive fears. For example, people with intrusive horrific religious images that are not triggered by any specific situation can't expose themselves to anything concrete that leads to obsessions; imagined exposure is the only choice. Chapter 8 discusses how you or your therapist might carry out imagined exposure if it appears that this would be helpful, in addition to exposure to the actual situations.

Remember that you will need to limit or eliminate rituals as you expose yourself to feared obsessive situations. Conducting ritual prevention is discussed in detail in Chapter 9. Please be sure to read Chapters 7 through 9 completely before returning to Chapter 7 to actually begin treatment.

Where To Start

If you have more than one hierarchy or theme behind your obsessive fears, it is usually best to begin with the one that interferes most in your life right now. If you choose an easier one, you are more likely to feel frustrated at the slow speed of your progress. Attacking your most persuasive fears first lets you feel great relief from anxiety and other unpleasant emotions without too long a wait.

So, choose the list of situations that upset you most and begin by selecting the easiest item on that list. This item should still make you uncomfortable even to think about. You may, of course, work on exposure to more than one item or hierarchy at once, but it is important that you not confuse yourself in this process. It is a far better idea to allow yourself the experience of some immediate, focused success. If you try desperately to eliminate all your fears at once, you'll only be setting yourself up for disappointment.

First, you must figure out how to expose yourself directly to a specific situation so that your fear has a chance to decrease. The process of reducing anxiety (and other negative emotions) during prolonged exposure is called "habituation," or "extinction." It is very much like the process by which your sense of smell adapts to an unpleasant odor, or the way you adjust to—and sometimes even stop hearing— initially distracting sounds, like an expressway near home. Somehow mental awareness of the unpleasantness of such circumstances decreases with time; you simply get used to it. The distraction does not always go away completely, but it becomes easier to cope with. Through a similar process, obsessive fears will provoke less anxiety if a person with OCD learns to tolerate them long enough to allow habituation to occur.

What To Do During Exposure

For those with obsessions of dirtiness or "contamination" from certain objects, exposure to those objects should be as complete as possible. That means touching the object to your hands—all over, not just the finger tips—to your face, your hair, and any other body part that you find you tend to try to protect from contamination. In some cases, we have asked people to sleep with the item that bothers them. You should also touch the item freely to other places or objects you have tried to keep "clean" or uncontaminated. The more completely you expose yourself and your clean things to the source of contamination, the more effective will be the exposure treatment in reducing your fear or discomfort in the long run.

The woman who feared glass slivers was asked to mix together the clothes she had kept separate in two different closets, since one held the "uncontaminated" clothing and the other the clothes that had been, or might have been, exposed to glass. Another woman, who used to try to keep her right hand "clean" while she used the left to touch "dirty" things, was asked to be sure she did the exposure with the "clean" hand. This is naturally very frightening to carry out, but very important. One patient described how she did her homework for the day—touching toilet flushers, stall door handles, sinks, faucets, and door handle on the way out. She then rubbed her hands together and on her face, wallet, pens, and money which she previously had tried to keep clean.

Experience suggests that when exposures are only partially completed, OCD symptoms tend to return after a period of time. It is therefore critical to eventually confront the *most feared* situations, even when exposure seems excessive for "normal" people. For example, one woman avoided using restrooms for fear of contracting a venereal disease, especially herpes or AIDS. She especially avoided the container for disposal of used tampons and sanitary napkins. When asked to touch the container and then her face, purse, etc., she complained that other women didn't usually do this. But she agreed that most could do so if necessary and understood that she needed to be able to touch *anything* in the restroom to be totally free of her fear. She touched the container, as requested, and eventually used bathrooms at work and in public places with ease.

For those with checking or repeating rituals, it is also important to carry out exposures as completely as possible. One patient always checked the silverware, glass, and plate he was about to use before eating. We asked him to turn his head away when he took these items from the drawer or cupboard, and to put food on the utensil without looking (as much as possible without spilling of course). Eventually, he was asked to deliberately leave a spot on his plate or cup and eat from it anyway. That allowed him a more complete habituation to the idea of "dirty" utensils, and to the possibility of health problems which he feared. His fears eased with time, continued exposures, and continued health.

Duration

For how long should you expose yourself to each situation on your selected hierarchy? As noted in the discussion of research about exposure therapy (Chapter 5), no one knows exactly how long a time period is best for exposure. What is most important is that the time be long enough to allow the person to feel noticeably more comfortable at the end of the exposure than at the beginning. The rule is to stop when you feel noticeably better, not when you still feel very bad. The amount of time is usually between 30 minutes and two hours for those who are fearful of things or objects they can directly touch. These are usually people with washing or cleaning rituals.

For those with checking, repeating, or other types of rituals, it may be impossible to remain in the disturbing situation for very long because it just doesn't last that long. A man who fears coming into contact with chemicals that might cause blindness can sit down and hold a bottle of ammonia or Draino for any length of time. Ideally, he should hold it until he feels his discomfort decrease by half or more. If such a decrease seems to take more than one or two hours, he might consider stopping that day's exposure when he notices at least some decline in discomfort. But someone who fears a burglar breaking into his home and worries about how he locked the door can only lock it once, taking a few seconds to do this. To expose himself to the obsessive fear, he must walk or drive away from the house and remain away until he feels he has grown a bit used to the situation and his urge to check is less. If he were to stay in the actual situation— in front of the door, or repeating the locking process—he would be allowing himself to check, which would defeat the purpose of the exposure.

We should note that we have treated a few individuals whose discomfort did not decline after exposure for several hours or even a day or two. Eventually, however, the tension reduced and the person was able to notice improvement. If you find that two hours is not sufficient, stick it out a little longer. The goal of freedom from obsessive fears and compulsive rituals is worth the wait.

In general, you want to expose yourself to a situation from your hierarchy at least once daily for as many minutes or hours as you need to allow discomfort to decline. It is a good idea to set aside two hours per day for this purpose. The actual exposure may last longer, since you will not be doing your rituals to reduce discomfort. The important part of the exposure is that you feel at least some discomfort, and that you learn to tolerate this until it becomes less disturbing. The more discomfort you are able to tolerate without resorting to rituals, the more rapidly you will be able to overcome your fears. Begin with the lowest items and progress to the next step as soon as you feel yourself becoming more relaxed with the previous one.

Repeat exposure sessions until you feel that you are ready to move to the next item on the hierarchy. You may spend only a single session on one item, or even include more than one item in the session if it goes easily and well. Another situation may require three or four sessions until the decrease in discomfort is really noticeable. If you find that one situation is taking a long time to become manageable, you might consider going past it to a higher item. Sometimes the contrast will help you think of the lower item as easier than you originally thought. And sometimes you may have underestimated the difficulty of a particular situation in creating your hierarchy. If progress is slow in one type of situation or hierarchy (for example, fear of chemicals), you can switch your focus temporarily to another one (for example, leaving objects lying around in others' way) where you may progress more rapidly. When you return your attention to the original hierarchy, it may even seem easier to you.

If you work on your exposure situations almost daily, you will probably see very noticeable improvement within a few weeks. Often people feel considerable decreases in discomfort after one or two weeks of daily exposure. How long it will take *you* to feel much less anxious in all your problem situations depends on the degree of initial anxiety you feel, as well as the degree to which your fears have generalized to many situations. Obviously, many hierarchies require more time for full habituation of fear to occur. Be sure to break your exposure work down into small and concentrated segments, so that you can see progress in certain areas even when many of your OCD symptoms persist.

General Behavioral Treatment Results

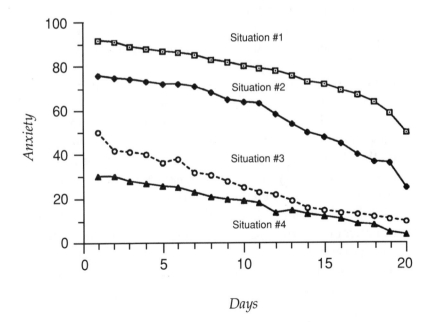

Tolerating Anxiety

Anxiety is inevitable as you confront your most feared situations. It's a necessary part of the healing process; habituation only occurs in face of the thing that's feared. But that doesn't mean you have to suffer. There are some specific coping strategies both you and your family can use to help ease the tension. You may already be familiar with many of these, and have found comfort in them. But some natural coping strategies tend to do more harm than good.

Distraction

Perhaps we should first discuss what *not* to do. Research suggests that when people with OCD attempt to distract themselves from a feared situation, they make exposure treatment even *harder* on themselves. Their anxiety level does not decline as rapidly during the exposure session, or between one session and the next, as it does for those who pay attention. This is probably akin to what the airplane phobic person experiences when flying frequently on business. He is exposed often to his fearful situation, but never seems to become more comfortable with flying. Why does habituation not occur in such an exposure situation? Probably because many phobic people try very hard to distract themselves: they take a tranquilizing pill or have a few drinks before and on the plane, they strike up a conversation with the stranger next to them, they read the magazines or attempt to do paperwork, they watch the movie or listen to the music on a radio headset. Never do they allow themselves to really pay full attention to the flight itself, to the noises of the engine, the occasional bumps in the air, and the other cues that frighten them. In such cases, distraction amounts to avoidance of the feared situation. It does *not* represent direct exposure to feared cues. Remember: it is important that in exposing yourself, you *feel* the fear!

During planned exposure periods, then, try hard to pay attention to all aspects of the situation, particularly those which are frightening or disturbing. Of course, this makes exposure more difficult. Just keep in mind that the immediate and long-term payoff is much greater for those willing to tolerate the anxiety. It will decrease on its own if you let it play itself out.

Happily, there are some coping strategies that can make anxiety easier to manage and still permit full exposure to the feared situation. These are not proven methods, but they have appeared helpful in our clinical observation.

Coping Strategies—Logical Argument

When anxiety is only moderate in intensity, perhaps 40 to 60 on the scale, it may be helpful to use logical arguments with yourself in facing the feared situation. For example, if you have a fear of "contamination," you might try to recall what you already know about the contaminant and how dangerous it is. The woman who feared slivers of glass reminded herself that even if a sliver had gotten into clothes (already unlikely), it was extremely unlikely that it could cause more than minor damage. She thought about a friend of hers, a very good mother, who was not at all concerned about broken glass around her children. She recalled that she herself had not worried about it a few years before and that her own mother, careful as she was, was never alarmed by this. She recalled getting glass in her hand and bleeding a few years before, without any consequences more unpleasant than a small cut that healed easily. In using these recollections, she was reminding herself of the obvious fact that her fears were unfounded. That allowed her to continue to expose herself and her daughter to normal activities that involved the possibility of broken glass.

In reminding yourself of the low risk involved in most obsessive feared situations, however, do not pretend that there is *no* risk. Estimate the probability of harm as accurately as you can, with whatever information is available. It is important to accept the realistic idea that there is *some* risk, even though it is extremely small. You might allow yourself to imagine the risky consequences in detail if these are uppermost in your mind. Show yourself that *even if* the worst case occurs, you are unlikely to suffer serious harm. We will talk about this further in the next chapter. Persons with OCD who reassure themselves that a situation does not really present *any* risk are merely using a different form of avoidance. As we know by now, this will not lead to a reduction in discomfort.

Coping Strategies—Self-Talk

Just as you can talk yourself through illogical fears, you can use self-talk to correct illogical conclusion-jumping. When people with OCD see elements of their obsessive fear in a situation, they often jump to immediate and catastrophic conclusions about the consequences of exposure. It is as if mere awareness of the feared context leads to an *automatic* thought about how dangerous, repugnant, sinful, etc. it is. If you tend to make such leaps before you realize what's happening, try to identify the form these thoughts take. Once you can identify the fear-raising phrase, you can counteract it with an appropriate, positive, logical statement. For example, someone who fears AIDS may find him- or herself thinking: "That spot there on my shirt—it looks brown and it *could be* dried blood! *What if* it's blood from someone with AIDS, like the woman at work whose brother is dying of AIDS? *Suppose* it came from her. *Oh my God* ! This is *terrible*. How do

I get rid of it? What else has touched it?" The automatic and irrational jump to conclusions in this thought process is noted in italics. To correct this thought process, you might say to yourself, "*What if* doesn't mean this has happened. It *could* be dried blood, but it could be a lot of other things, like dried pizza sauce from lunch. And anyway, dried blood is hardly the same as getting AIDS. Come on now, you're way ahead of yourself." You want to prevent yourself from catastrophizing so quickly that you assume danger (harm, evil, etc.) before you've even thought about the situation realistically. Thus it's important to plan a helpful set of counter-phrases before anxiety sets in.

The following chart of fear-increasing and reducing statements may be helpful:

Not Helpful	Helpful
Uh oh! I've done it now!	Just wait a while longer. Nothing has really changed.
I'll *never* get used to this.	I got used to the last situation. This will eventually get easier.
I can't stand this anxiety. Oh my God! *What if* … ! How Awful!	What exactly am I worried about?
This is *perfectly* safe.	There might be *some* risk, but I'll have to accept it to get over my fears. This *could* conceivably be dangerous, but it is very unlikely and so I'm better off *assuming* it's safe.

Supposing (the feared consequence) actually happens; I'll never forgive myself.	What's the real probability that my fears are justified? I usually "suppose" more than is really true.
Good mothers (Catholics, fathers, etc.) don't . . .	What would (trusted friend or relative) think or do in my place now? How did I used to think or feel about this before I became obsessive?

Coping Strategies—Relaxation

Formal relaxation training has long been a cornerstone of anxiety-reduction programs. It involves learning techniques—from deep breathing to visualization to meditation—to calm tensed muscles and ease other symptoms of anxiety. This process is a major component of one behavioral treatment technique known as systematic desensitization. In this method, deep muscle relaxation is paired with brief exposures to mildly fear-evoking situations. It is used most commonly for treating simple phobias, such as fears of dogs, elevators, heights, etc. We noted in Chapter 5 that desensitization was generally too slow a method for reducing obsessive fears, especially when it did not include prevention of rituals. However, relaxation can ease the anxiety connected with particular fears, and may allow you enough comfort to enter difficult exposure situations. Most sufferers of OCD can benefit from the physically calming effects of deep breathing.

Deep breathing is something you can practice throughout the day; many insomniacs learn to use it at night. It can help you move on to the next level of your hierarchy, and ease the actual tension of an exposure session. If you would like to learn more complex deep muscle relaxation, there are several good books available on this topic. They are listed in Appendix A under "Relaxation."

To practice breathing control:

1. Lean back in a comfortable chair and put one hand on your chest and the other on your stomach. Breathe in through your nose, pulling the air all the way into your lungs so the hand on your stomach moves but the one on your chest remains relatively still. Exhale through your nose naturally. Next, breathe even deeper, so you feel the hand on your chest move up slightly after the hand on your stomach does, and back down after the hand on your stomach moves back down. You might imagine that when you inhale, you are blowing up a balloon in your stomach, which deflates when you release the air.

2. Next concentrate on slowing down your breathing, using a counting pattern: In - two - three, out - two - three. Breathe as slowly as you can without holding your breath or straining. Notice as you practice that you tend to feel calmer and more comfortable.

3. Try to practice this twice or more a day for 5 to 10 minutes each time. It is especially helpful to practice when you are driving the car, or watching TV, or reading a newspaper, so you can learn to relax in many everyday situations. Notice that the more you practice, the more even and slow your breathing becomes in general, and the easier it is to calm yourself when you feel mildly uncomfortable.

Coping Strategies—Paradoxical Intention

When anxiety in the exposure situation is fairly high, perhaps 70 or more, it is unlikely that logical self-talk (or relaxation techniques) will be helpful. Most people are too tense to think clearly about the feared situation. A better coping strategy may be to allow yourself to think about your fear coming true—in its *worst* possible form. This is a technique known as "paradoxical intention" (it was discussed briefly in Chapter 5). It is not avoidance, but another aspect of exposure: exposure to the feared consequences themselves. The idea is that you exaggerate your fearful ideas until they become so absurd that you have to laugh at them, or at least see how unlikely or far-fetched your fears really are.

One man was following his exposure program and locked his car door without checking the parking brake, the gearshift, or the lock. He then walked away. As his anxiety rose, he imagined that all three things were done improperly and that the car began to roll backwards. In fact, he imagined that it rolled over many people, including a large group of children who were flattened like pancakes. A thief then stopped the unlocked car at the foot of the hill and stole it, thus removing the "murder weapon." The car owner, a religious Catholic, tried to confess the "crime," but the police refused to listen to his story and so he never got the punishment he felt he deserved. When he imagined going to the priest of his parish to confess, he was told he could not be absolved of a crime he did not commit. Thus, the man died "in sin" and could not go to heaven.

This scenario was dreamed up by the OCD patient himself; it was not created by the therapist who treated him. If you decide to use paradoxical intention in coping with anxiety, it is essential that your scenario come from your own ideas about what might happen, rather than someone else's. Be honest; be creative. This method has proved quite useful in helping people recognize the absurdity of their fears, even when they are quite anxious. It is very much akin to imagined exposure (which will be discussed in the next chapter), although it is not used in as systematic or prolonged a manner.

Coping Strategies—Humor

The above scene suggests that yet another useful way to cope with anxiety during exposure is humor. Laughter helps cut tension and put things in manageable perspective. You may find it easier to laugh at a situation if someone else is present (a therapist, family member, or friend, preferably *with* a sense of humor): an audience. It is difficult to generate funny ideas without someone to respond to them, especially when you are quite anxious to begin with. Of course, it is important that the humorous ideas not ridicule people with OCD, but rather poke fun at the ridiculousness of the situations they find themselves in.

Driving over people and flattening them like pancakes is one example of a real fear exaggerated to a cartoonish extent. With one woman who was fearful of spreading germs from public restrooms, the therapist joked that touching toilet seats in the college restrooms and then eating in the cafeteria could wipe out most of the student body. The headlines in the paper would read: "Therapist and OCD Patient Pose Major Public Health Hazard" or "Students Slain by Toilet Seat Germs." The patient was invited to generate yet more absurd headlines. Germs could be described as marching with their little bodies in uniform, carrying muskets, machine guns, or swords depending on the client's imagination. Whenever a feared situation can be seen as absurd or ridiculous, humor can have a prominent place in alleviating discomfort.

Coping Strategies—Call a Friend

When exposure proves difficult and you're tempted to ritualize, talk to a trusted friend, family member, or therapist *before* giving in to the urge to do compulsions. Friends can be asked ahead of time to tell you clearly *not* to ritualize but to stick it out. They can help support you emotionally long enough to allow anxiety to lessen a little, giving you the strength to face the fear longer. Adopting someone else's world view for a short period can help put your unreasonable fears in perspective. Sometimes just talking through a fear and finding support is enough to ease the tension.

One patient found that telling a good friend what she had to do during an upcoming exposure period (touch faucets and toilet flushers) was "good reality testing." The friend told her that she "wouldn't think twice about doing it." This can backfire, of course, if you tell a finicky friend what you need to do and he or she tells you that it sounds like "cruel and unusual punishment!" Select the friend carefully; it should be someone you consider "easygoing."

Other Coping Methods

One very insightful OCD patient suggested the following additional strategies she relied on to cope with fear. Once she experienced an anxiety decline following exposure, she derived faith from the memory of success when the going got tough later. You can remind yourself firmly, "Discomfort will lessen if I just wait it out. If I wait another hour (another few hours, another day), I know from experience that I'll feel better. I can handle this a little longer." You already know the abstract fact that fear habituates with time; use your own history to remind yourself of its real application.

This patient used another form of positive self-talk to ease her anxiety when fear took hold. She reminded herself that the fear was "just my OCD acting up," to clarify the unreasonableness of the fear. Of course the fear *feels* real, but successful treatment of OCD is based on learning that feelings of discomfort cannot be trusted when they refer to your obsessive thoughts, images, or impulses. Remind yourself that this is your "illness"; that the danger isn't *really* happening, you just feel or think that it is. The patient who described this method told herself *"My* problem isn't Christ's attitudes toward me as a sinful person; it's just my OCD."

Avoidance

As described in the beginning of this section, you must watch for any form of avoidance during your daily exposure session. You may find it helpful to have someone around who can tell you when your behavior seems "odd" for most people in a situation (such as touching a doorknob only with your fingertips or only on the "cleaner" parts). Partial exposure can only produce partial benefits that won't last. This means that you must experience *real* discomfort by touching or confronting all parts of the avoided objects or situations; protecting yourself will only prolong the process or make it unproductive.

When Is Exposure Dangerous?

In some situations, exposure presents a realistic element of danger. For example, there are times when not checking at all allows the real possibility of fire, since others besides the person with OCD use the appliances in question. That does *not* mean exposure is a bad idea; on the contrary, you need to learn that some element of risk is a normal part of life. Still, you may wonder where the line is between reasonable and dangerous risks. When is it dangerous to touch red spots that might be blood and when is it safe? How much use of a pesticide could be considered harmful? In keeping kosher, exactly how careful must an orthodox Jew be in his or her own kitchen? When does repeated confession in the Catholic church amount to an OCD ritual? Clearly, there are not hard and fast rules one can apply to such situations. Real life cannot always be divided into safe and unsafe situations.

When there is a *legitimate* question of what is acceptable or nondangerous behavior, it might be a good idea to consult an expert in the field. However, you must be careful that this is not a ritualistic effort to seek yet more reassurance about safety. The expert should know *why* you're asking so specifically: you might describe yourself as a very cautious person who sometimes exaggerates the risk involved. Make sure the expert understands that you want specifications on something you're already *very* careful about. General cautions, after all, may lead you to avoid the situation altogether. Remember that one of your main tasks in treatment is to confront feared obsessive situations. Even if your fears involve causing harm to yourself or others, exposure requires you to take more risks.

How Can Family Members and Friends Help?

People with OCD can derive considerable help from understanding family members and friends, provided each knows how to be helpful to the other. Many tasks in the treatment—from the construction of hierarchies to support in confronting the items on those hierarchies—become easier with a close advisor's help. The key to effective consultation and support is that it be given in a *non-judgmental* manner. The person with OCD must be allowed to make all final decisions about what kind of exposure to use and how to do it. It can be difficult to maintain a neutral attitude, but if family members and friends remember that the OCD sufferer knows his or her *own* emotions, abilities, and problem best, it may be easier.

The OCD sufferer can also make it easier for others to help. Keep in mind that outsiders (even therapists or family members) cannot possibly know what your discomfort feels like or how strong it is on any given occasion. They can only guess from indirect evidence they can see but not feel. So the afflicted person must tell or show outsiders what goes on inside. In other words, say how you feel!

If a family member can't refrain from making negative comments or using a critical or sarcastic tone of voice, it is best that he or she stay out of the treatment program altogether. More damage might be done than progress made, no matter how good the original intention. Progress can also be hindered by someone at the opposite extreme, who shows too much concern or becomes overly involved in the exposure treatment. Remember, it is the person with OCD who needs to decide to do the exposures in order to benefit most from them. Family members help when they act as consultants and offer *neutral* observations and concerned support without adding emotional intensity to an already tension-fraught situation.

One of our patients offered the following list of comments she received during her treatment: she separated them into helpful and not helpful. The latter usually came from her critical mother, and sometimes from her husband when he was tired and impatient. Notice the tone of dismissal in the "Not Helpful" column, and the willingness to listen and understand in the "Helpful" column.

Not Helpful	Helpful
Oh, that's ridiculous.	OK, let's talk about it.
There's nothing there.	Did you actually see any pieces of glass?
Forget about it.	Sit a moment and relax.
You're slipping.	Why don't you wait a bit and see how you feel then?
Not this again!	It's *not* OK to wash just to make sure. That will only get you into trouble.

I don't want to hear about it.	I understand how you might feel that way.
I thought you got over that.	Remember how calm you felt last time?
There's nothing there.	Did you actually see any pieces of glass?
You're not trying hard enough.	I know this is hard for you.
It doesn't make any difference.	What would someone else do in this situation?
That's crazy.	What are the realistic chances that someone might get hurt?

Summary

We have suggested strategies in this chapter for developing a hierarchy: your list of increasingly difficult exposure situations, organized according to the type of disaster feared, or the type of concrete situation that provokes discomfort. Your hierarchy is your agenda for gradually progressing exposure treatments. Some anxiety is a normal part of the exposure experience, although it will decrease in intensity throughout your exposure sessions. Methods for coping with high levels of anxiety encountered during exposure include logical discussion, using relaxation techniques, exaggerating feared outcomes until they seem absurd, and finding something humorous about the exposure situation. By contrast, distraction from the exposure or avoidance of aspects of the confrontation will cause long-term difficulties in becoming comfortable with feared obsessive situations. Consultation with an expert may be helpful where it is genuinely difficult to know if there is actual danger. But you should be careful not to let such consultation allow you to avoid confronting your obsessive fears.

8

Reducing Obsessive Fears: Imagined Exposure

The previous chapter discussed strategies for conducting direct confrontation with situations or objects that provoke obsessive fears. This chapter is written for those people who, in addition to direct exposure, are also likely to benefit from *imagining* confrontation with discomfort-producing situations. Many of the suggestions offered in Chapter 7 will also apply to imagined exposure.

Imagined exposure involves constructing detailed mental pictures of your feared obsessive situations, and then going through these scenes in your imagination as if they were really happening around you. Once you have perfected your visualization skills, imagined confrontation can be a powerful and constructive experience. As in direct exposure, imagined exposure starts with the least disturbing image and progresses to more disturbing scenes as anxiety and discomfort are reduced. This chapter will address many of the questions you'll have about imagined exposure, beginning with a discussion of when it is appropriate, and moving on to explain how to construct scenes and how to implement the exposure process. Note that conducting imagined exposure may be difficult if you have multiple obsessive fears and cannot decide which aspects of your fear to include in each scene. If you find the following suggestions unmanageable, you may need to consult with a professional therapist to help plan your treatment.

Who Requires Imagined Exposure?

Individuals with certain types of obsessive fears appear to benefit more than others from treatment by imagined exposure. First, there are those obsessions that *occur* in imagery: that is, the obsession is actually a specific mental image that makes you upset. Examples include one woman's image of the devil raping the Virgin Mary, or one man's image of himself stabbing his child. In these cases, a clear image appeared in the person's mind that was horrifying and proved very difficult to dispel. The images frequently appeared "out of the blue" without apparent relation to any particular situation. In such cases, conjuring up the feared image mentally is close to direct exposure, and thus very effective.

Second, imagined exposure can help you if disastrous consequences dominate your obsessive ideas. This is particularly true if the disasters don't readily come to mind during direct confrontation with feared situations (as described in Chapter 7). One example is a fear of running over someone on the highway, accompanied by images of the dead body, police searching for the hit-and-run driver, etc. Another example is one woman's obsession of looking at other women's breasts, especially when they were wearing tight or revealing clothing, and at men's genital areas. Her urge to look was accompanied by ideas that the person would notice that she was looking or notice her anxiety and would reject her. In such a case, direct exposure to the feared cues would be awkward! Imagined exposure offers a more practical form of confrontation to a whole range of socially uncomfortable cues.

A third type of situation that may require imagined exposure is where obsessive fears are hard to reproduce in practice. For example, for someone who is disturbed by "contamination" from dead animals, it isn't always easy to locate a dead animal that fits the description. A woman who feared the coincidence of a light shining in her dog's eyes (so they glinted red) when it was 13 minutes before or 13 minutes after the hour had a similar problem. This reminded her of "the devil" and led her to repeat whatever she had just done, to neutralize any harm that might have come to one of her children or to the dog. Because this event happened infrequently and unpredictably, it was more easily confronted in imagination than in reality.

How To Construct a Scene

Just as in direct exposure, imagined exposure should be arranged in sequence from least to most disturbing image. If only one kind of image bothers you, you'll have no need for such a hierarchy. But most Obsessive Compulsive Disorder (OCD) sufferers experience some variation in the types of obsessive situation they face. The easiest way to approach multiple fears is to organize them into a short list, ranking them by degree of discomfort. If you can find common themes among the cues and situations on your list, you will probably be able to keep your work down to creating three to five separate scenes. You'll be able to include many disturbing cues in a single scenario.

Scenes for imagined exposure are not like snapshots, but more like a movie or perhaps a nightmare. They re-create a series of events that happen one after another, all having to do with a specific obsessive idea. You can replay such "videos" in your mind until they no longer disturb you. The images should be as vivid as possible, much like in your dreams, so you'll need to imagine a lot of detail. To make the scenes very clear, you'll want to include the following components:

Sensory Experiences

How would the external setting of this scene affect you if this were a real situation? Think about all your senses. For example, you need to become aware of 1) what you are seeing (the color of clothing, the look on someone's face, movements of objects, etc.); 2) what you can smell (odor of a pesticide, smell of your grandmother's musty closet, etc.); 3) what you hear (other people's words, the crash of a car, etc.); 4) what you feel or touch (someone touching you on your arm, heat from a fire, the smooth surface of a toilet seat, etc.); and even 5) what you taste (a bitter taste in your mouth, your tongue going dry, etc.). This is the detail that convinces your body an experience is real.

Emotional Responses

What feelings result from the sensory cues you perceive? For example, while imagining the scene, you might experience fear, anxiety, guilt, anger, irritation, sadness, embarrassment, shame, or surprise, alone, or in any combination. You might also have some positive feelings, such as gladness or pride. Acknowledge and allow yourself to experience all of your feelings. The most effective imagined exposure session will permit you to confront the most disturbing feelings surrounding an obsessive situation.

Internal Physiological Reactions

What happens to your body as you face the situation and go through your various emotional responses? You may feel your heart beating fast, your muscles tense (especially in your face), your knees weaken, or your breathing quicken. Different emotions often cause different physical reactions: sadness about losing someone might give you a lump in your throat; embarrassment might make your face flush hotly. Think about your typical responses, and recall how they feel during your scene.

Behavior

What do you actually *do* in the scene? Your actions should appear as clearly as possible. Feel your legs move as you walk toward something, or your hand move as you pick something up. What do you say to others in the image? Obviously, your behavior will be closely associated with your sensory reactions (sight, smell, hearing, and especially touch).

Thoughts and Ideas

What goes through your mind about what is happening? Your answer is linked to the meaning the situation has for you, especially the disasters you fear. For example, the woman (described in Chapter 7) who feared that glass slivers might be eaten by her daughter believed that this would prove her a bad mother. Failure to check for glass or to clean an area that might have glass meant she would be to blame if her daughter came to harm. She was less concerned about other people's reaction to her neglect, even her own mother's reaction, than her own sense of conscience and God's view of her and her "sins." In her imagined scene, this woman needed to include thoughts about being neglectful and about what a mother "should" do in this situation. She could also have added the idea that she had sinned against God and deserved punishment.

You do not need to invent disasters in the scene; only include images that automatically occur to you. In addition, the scene should contain *no rituals*. Do not carry out or picture yourself carrying out any compulsive acts or thoughts which would reduce your fears artificially. These interfere with the habituation of your obsessive fears and will therefore actually hinder your progress. Stopping rituals is discussed further in Chapter 9.

Before thinking about the types of imagined scenes you might construct, make sure you understand the elements that go into establishing the *vividness* of the image. The above components all enhance the clarity of a scene. If you cannot imagine your scene as if it were real, it won't help you. Imagined exposure to a hazy image is more like reading a book about an experience than having it yourself. The scene should seem so real that it causes you almost as much discomfort in your imagined exposure as it does in real life. Don't put yourself *outside* the scene observing yourself; you want to be *in* the image at the present moment. Concentrate on seeing, hearing, and feeling everything that goes on around you and in your mind, unpleasant as it may be.

Examples of Imagined Exposure Scenes

It's a good idea to run through one or two practice scenes before evoking the situations in your hierarchy. These scenes will help most if they are emotionally neutral or positive in tone.

For example, try to put yourself back to an earlier birthday party, or a day in school, to perfect your skill in imagined scene setting. If you have difficulty achieving vividness or clarity with these scenes, you might try practicing *imagery* first with other more neutral experiences. For example, picture yourself using a sharp knife to cut a lemon in half and focus on the sensations involved in the process: the smooth handle of the knife, the feel of the blade sliding through first the lemon peel and then the softer insides, the bright yellow color of the fruit, the distinctive odor of lemon juice, and its very tart taste as you lick a slice of the lemon.

If you cannot easily conjure up emotional reactions to the obsessive image, allow yourself to think of several events you can recall clearly that caused strong emotional reactions. You might recall how you felt when your child was born, or when you just learned that someone close to you had died, or in a situation where there was very real danger to you or someone else. Such practice sessions can help you feel more able to experience the emotions that disturb you in your obsessive images.

The example that follows will help you see the order and the level of detail that make a good imagined scene most effective. The patient who constructed this scene feared *hitting and killing a pedestrian* in his car and being arrested for a crime. Imagined exposure provided him a confrontation with the most feared consequences in his obsessive fears. Notice the attention he gives to physical detail and feeling, and see how that detail helps make the scene real.

Example

I'm in the car driving on Maple Road and it's pretty busy. It's a rainy day, which always makes me more uncomfortable because it's harder to see clearly. I can hear the sound of the car wheels on the wet pavement. I'm on my way to an appointment to make a sale, and of course I'm a little late as usual. There are a lot of pedestrians trying to cross the street because there are a lot of shops along this section of the road. One of them, an old lady, is on my right and she steps off the sidewalk onto the highway. I hate that. I wish she'd cross at the light when I'm stopped instead of when the car is moving. I can see her dress—it's blue and sort of dowdy looking—and she's carrying her purse and a shopping bag with a handle, the kind made of thick clear plastic with flowers on it. I can also see someone trying to cross the road from my left, headed for my car. It's a man in a suit, but I don't have time to look at him carefully.

The two of them are walking out into the street. I'm afraid that I won't see them well enough or they won't see me and they'll walk in front of my car. The guy on the left keeps coming, so I turn my head in his direction and he waits till I go by. But I've lost track of where the old lady went. I can feel myself perspiring and my hand gripping the steering wheel so the knuckles are white. Where did the old lady go? Where is she? I wasn't paying attention to her when I looked over at the man and now I don't see her.

Uh oh. I hit a bump with my right wheel. A hole in the road, I'm hoping, but maybe it wasn't a hole in the road. Maybe I hit the old lady! Oh my God! Suppose it was the old lady? I look up to check the rear view mirror, but it's a little out of position so I can't see very well. I crane my neck to see better. The rear windshield is covered with rain and all I can see are vague shapes behind me. I've slowed down and a car behind me is honking and probably wants me to go faster. But what about the old lady? Could I have hit her? I didn't see her in front of the car but I looked away for a second and maybe she stepped in front of me and I didn't notice. What was that bump? Did it feel like a body? I'm not sure. It felt like a hole in the road and the wheel jumped up after that, but it could have been a body! I've got to keep the car moving, the guy behind keeps honking. I can't stop here, but I've got to find out about that lady.

I go down to the next corner, about four blocks from the spot where I might have hit the woman. I try to make a right turn so I can return to the "scene of the crime," but it's blocked off by construction—they've got the road partly dug up for new pipes or something. It seems to take forever to turn around. Then I realize I can't go back up

Maple Road because it's one way against me. This is taking forever. I'm getting later and later for my sale. I drive on further and try again, but this time fire trucks block the side street. I'm getting more and more anxious and worried. Now I hear police sirens behind me and that really makes me worry about whether I hit her. They're coming for me! They stop several blocks back. I can't see anything except the houses and the street around me. I feel terrible—my stomach is upset and I'm hot. I feel sick. I keep remembering the feel of the wheel when I bumped and trying to figure out if it was a hole or a body!

It seems like every time I try to turn to go back to the "scene of the crime," I can't go in that direction. There must be a way but I can't seem to find it. I have to get to my appointment, but I keep remembering the image of the old woman and the feeling of the car wheel bumping on the road. Now I hear more sirens behind me but I can't tell how far behind. Maybe they're back at the intersection I'm worrying about. Maybe they'll come for me because I really did hit her!

[MOVE THE CLOCK FORWARD; YOU GO TO YOUR APPOINTMENT AND RETURN HOME.]

At home, I hear on the news that there was a hit-and-run accident on Maple Road at about the time that I passed through the intersection. A woman was hit and I'm convinced that I did it. It really happened. I really hit her!

[AT THIS POINT, THE DISASTER SHOULD MATCH WHAT THE PERSON FEARS. FOR SOME PEOPLE, THIS MIGHT MEAN THAT THE POLICE COME TO ARREST THEM AND PUT THEM IN JAIL; FOR OTHERS, IT MIGHT MEAN THAT THEY ARE NEVER QUITE SURE WHETHER THEY WERE RESPONSIBLE AND THEY HAVE TO LIVE WITH THIS UNCERTAINTY FOREVER.]

There is a knock on the door. When I answer it, there are two cops standing there, a man and a woman. They ask me whether I'm John Doe, and I nod. They say I'm under arrest for a hit-and-run accident and give the time and place and tell me that my car with license plate #234CDS was identified as the car that struck an old woman. I can't believe this is happening to me! I can feel the blood drain from my face and I feel dizzy and nauseated. I can hear the male cop reading me my rights and I see the woman shaking her head and frowning, as if she disapproves of me and is disgusted by the whole situation. She mutters under her breath something about a "defenseless old woman." I can sense her loathing me. I ask what happened to the woman and they say she's in the hospital in critical condition. They tell me I have to come with them to the police station and that I should call my lawyer. I'm petrified of what will happen to me, but I can't stop picturing the old woman and thinking about how I hit her and how she's going to die because of me. I might already have killed her! All because I wasn't paying attention at the intersection. I looked away. It's my fault. I'm going to go to jail!

[THE ENTIRE SCENE IS REPEATED TWO OR THREE TIMES DURING A SESSION OF IMAGINED EXPOSURE. IN EACH RUN-THROUGH, THE PATIENT FOCUSES IN ON THE DETAILS THAT CAUSE THE MOST DISCOMFORT. EVENTUALLY, THE ANXIETY LEVEL WILL DECREASE, ALTHOUGH THE EXTERNAL DETAILS OF THE SCENE REMAIN THE SAME.]

The above example demonstrates how to build an imaginary scene that incorporates typical OCD fear/guilt/discomfort cues. Note the concrete environmental cues that could be seen, heard, and felt, as well as the carefully noted internal bodily sensations, physical behaviors, emotional reactions, and thoughts and ideas. Details were included (the pattern of the woman's umbrella, the woman police officer's expression) to keep the image as clear as possible. The disaster that the person with OCD feared (being arrested) was included in the image, even though it is a situation that would really upset *anyone*. It is important to realize that you can become accustomed to even very unpleasant or frightening images if they are repeated long enough.

How To Conduct the Imagined Exposure

Begin your session by finding a comfortable place to sit without being disturbed for at least one hour. Close your eyes to shut out the visual representation of the room. Begin to describe the scene chronologically, starting with visual details of the image and adding the other senses as you go. A good strategy for keeping yourself actively involved in the exposure image is to *tape record* your own voice during the session. Keep a recorder running as you describe the scene for yourself, painting the details as vividly as possible. This focuses your attention on the image, and keeps you from getting distracted by other events and thoughts that would allow you to avoid the most fearful parts of the scene. You can use the tape recording of the scene for playback later, either in that day's session or in future imagined sessions, to help you focus in on the image. You might, for instance, recognize a particular detail that rang true for you, and imagine it more thoroughly.

Although many people find the tape recorder helpful in these ways, some find themselves uncomfortable with it— they feel awkward in front of the microphone or find their own voice on tape strange and distracting. If this is true of you, you may be better off just imagining the scene or describing it aloud without the recorder.

The *duration* of the scene should depend, as in actual exposure, on how soon your discomfort declines when you imagine the scene. For most people, this will require 45 minutes to two hours in the beginning, but less as each scene is repeated. As with direct exposure, the rule is to keep imagining the most difficult parts of the scene until your discomfort decreases noticeably, preferably by at least a third. Waiting until you are aware of a significant improvement in your mood before stopping lets you learn that tolerating the image and your feelings of anxiety leads to eventual relief. The more you teach yourself to tolerate discomfort rather than to avoid or escape it, the more rapidly and completely you will overcome the domination of your obsessive ideas. Your goal is to be *able* to have unpleasant ideas occur to you from time to time, as all people do, without having these ideas upset you too much or take up all your time. This will only occur if you can let yourself *think* about fearful ideas that pop into your head without trying desperately to rid yourself of them. Imagined exposure allows you to teach yourself this important lesson.

Keeping track of discomfort is a good idea during exposure to the obsessive scene. (The anxiety scale of 0-100 described in Chapter 7 comes in handy here.) Writing down your anxiety level every five minutes or so lets you to see if it changes during the course of the exposure. It also allows you to see what parts of the scene cause you the most discomfort. These are, of course, the parts that you need to focus on most when you imagine and return to them in later sessions. Recording your discomfort at regular intervals will keep you aware of your reactions, so that you can decide on an ending point that is significantly lower than your highest level of discomfort. In deciding when to stop the scene, it is important to be sure your fear did not go down just because you concentrated on easier parts of the image.

How often to repeat a scene depends on the degree of anxiety it generates. Remember from the graph in Chapter 7 that with repeated exposure, you can expect your discomfort during an obsessive image to habituate. This means that the first time you picture the scene will be the hardest, but the second or third time your peak level of discomfort will probably lessen and less time will be required for anxiety to reduce. Sometimes progress is slow, but if you keep a record of your discomfort, you can usually see the change. Assume you will have to repeat each image at least once and maybe four or five times before you are ready to go on to the next more difficult one. This could mean as many as 20 to 25 imagined exposure periods; it may seem like a lot of work, but it's well worth the effort if it helps you rid yourself of the intense unpleasant feelings attached to your obsessive ideas.

Aids to Habituation

As mentioned in conjunction with actual exposure treatment, *humor* can also be a useful ally in imagined exposure. It should not divert attention from the uncomfortable aspects of the obsessive situation, but laughter can help make the uncomfortable feelings easier to tolerate. You'll probably find that it is easier to introduce humorous aspects to a scene later on, after you have already been through the image at least once or twice and feel more accustomed to the scene than you did at the beginning. Humor can help reduce anxiety or guilt more rapidly. Consider focusing on amusing aspects of the image if you find your discomfort reduces very slowly.

An example of humor would be picturing "contamination" from bathroom germs as a group of tiny little creatures, in absurd outfits, who march up your fingers to your hands and arms in time to a drum beaten by a member of the troupe—like a flea circus. This image does not avoid the idea of contamination, but adds visual silliness to fears that you already know to be unrealistic. In the police example, you might imagine the policeman and woman in comical ways, like Keystone Cops, although they should still keep their disapproving expressions since these were part of your obsessive concerns.

Summary

In this chapter, we have outlined some strategies for exposing yourself in imagination to your feared obsessive situations. These include concrete cues and feared disastrous consequences, as well as the internal physical and emotional responses that accompany them. Imagined exposure is most appropriate if your obsessions are actually images, especially horrific images, or if you focus heavily on feared disasters. Sometimes it is more convenient to carry out exposure in imagery than in reality. But don't use this as an excuse to avoid direct exposure to situations you really could expose yourself to.

A hierarchy of a few imagined scenes can be constructed for each type of obsessive fear, and exposure begins with the easier images. Maintaining and repeating vivid mental scenes are important until discomfort decreases noticeably. A tape recorder may facilitate the process and humor may be helpful in managing the level of fear and introducing a lighter perspective. Clear images of the feared cues and emotional reactions are important in allowing the exposure to have the most impact.

9

Stopping Rituals

Chapter 5 discussed treatment programs that combine exposure to obsessive feared situations with the blocking of rituals, a two-part method known as "exposure with response prevention" in scientific literature. Successful treatment for people with Obsessive Compulsive Disorder (OCD) requires *simultaneous* exposure and prevention of rituals. Chapters 7 and 8 have focused on how to expose yourself *directly* and in *imagination* to your obsessive fears. Now it's time to look at how to block both overt compulsive behaviors and mental rituals. It is crucial that you use the techniques described in this chapter along with those described in the previous two chapters.

Why isn't exposure to feared situations enough? Why is it necessary to also block the rituals? You might guess that compulsions would stop automatically as you work through exposures and feel your anxiety or discomfort decrease. In some cases of newly developed OCD, this might actually be the case. Once anxiety is reduced by exposure, rituals that began recently (within the past year), and that have a very specific purpose, might no longer feel necessary and then stop on their own.

But for most people with OCD, compulsions have been going on for well over a year, in some cases decades. Over this time, rituals become so habitual that they serve to relieve tension from many sources of worry besides the original obsessive fears. Whenever you are worried about anything (what other people might think about you, whether you'll pass an exam, etc.), you might find yourself wishing to wash your hands, check something, or repeat an action, even though the original reasons for washing or checking or repeating aren't even present. In this way, compulsions that develop for specific reasons come to serve the general function of reducing discomfort. Exposure alone might reduce the fear of particular obsessive situations, but it will have only a limited effect on the need (or habit) of doing compulsions.

Even if compulsions began only recently, it is still important to block them deliberately while exposing yourself to feared situations. Exposure is only useful to the extent that it allows you to fully experience the obsessive situation and associated discomfort. Only in this way can you learn that just *tolerating* the anxiety (guilt, etc.) without escaping it will reduce the discomfort. You'll slowly be able to view the situation more objectively and rationally. If rituals interrupt your obsessive fear prematurely, you cannot feel the anxiety decrease on its own. Rituals prevent you from seeing that a situation is not really dangerous and need not lead to anxiety. They also prevent you from developing more adaptive coping strategies for managing your fears (such as using logical self-talk to calm yourself, or humor, etc.).

In general, we believe it is best to strive for maximal reduction of rituals from the beginning. However, some people have difficulty maintaining their commitment under the stress of "cold turkey" ritual-stopping. Several methods of gradual ritual-reduction have been tested, and they are included here for those who prefer a more graduated approach. Clinical tests are still inconclusive as to which method is most effective. Of course, if cold turkey proves impractical and it's a choice between gradual reduction and none at all, any of the methods below would be a wise choice.

Gradual Methods for Reducing Rituals

Response Delay

Some researchers have used a modified method of ritual prevention, called "response delay," to help people with OCD decrease their compulsive behaviors. In this method, a person exposes him- or herself to a particular feared situation and then *delays* carrying out the compulsive actions for longer and longer periods of time. Sometimes delay is planned for a specific length of time, such as 10 minutes or 30 minutes or one hour. In other cases, the delay of the ritual is supposed to be "as long as possible." This method has been tried with a few individuals but has never been tested on large numbers of people or in comparison with other methods. It seems to be useful for those who can't carry out the more stringent methods described below. If this method proves your favorite, be careful not to use it as an excuse to continue ritualizing! An alcoholic who delays his drinking until after work can still ruin his life with alcohol. The idea behind response delay is to increase the delay steadily, so that eventually the ritual never occurs at all.

Ritual Restriction

A second gradual method of ritual reduction is to limit the time allowed for each ritual or the actions involved in each compulsion. For example, a person who took 45-minute showers might be asked to reduce them by five minutes every few days, until no more than 10 to 15 minutes were necessary. Or a man who handwashed for two minutes would be asked to wash 10 seconds less each time, working toward a normal 20-to-30 second time period. One way to accomplish such a reduction is to limit the specific actions a person is allowed to do. The handwasher might be asked not to wash each finger separately (as he'd been doing), thereby eliminating many seconds from his washing time. A woman who checked lists of daily planned activities would be allowed to examine her list from top to bottom only, eliminating the reverse direction check she was in the habit of doing. A man who repeated buttoning and unbuttoning his shirt four times could be told to decrease the repetitions on each button by one until after a few days it was down to no repetitions.

Selective Ritual Prevention

A third gradual method is to permit ritualizing in situations high on the fear hierarchy, but to eliminate rituals entirely following exposure to easier obsessive situations. This system is used in many exposure and response prevention programs involving progressive exposure to increasingly fearful circumstances. Rituals are allowed to continue for situations not yet included in planned exposure. Once the person begins to expose him- or herself to a new feared item on the list, however, *no* ritual of any kind is allowed in relation to that item afterwards. For example, suppose it is more difficult to lock the car than to lock the front door of the house. You would stop checking the front door lock once you had included leaving the house in your exposure work, but you would still be allowed to check the car door as often as desired. Later on in treatment, when the car has become a focus of exposure, you would stop checking in this situation too.

The method just described can be an effective strategy, and it may work well for you. Unfortunately, some people find it

difficult to decide when to allow rituals and when not because their anxiety fluctuates from day to day in the same
situation. It may actually make it harder to carry out ritual
prevention if you have to make a decision in each situation
about whether you can ritualize or not. Often it is easier in
the beginning of treatment to know that you cannot check at
all, than to try to decide when it is okay and when it is not.
Such discriminations may become easier later on, when fear
or discomfort is already somewhat eased as a result of exposure.

Another problem with the partial response prevention
method is that rituals allowed in some situations may serve
to relieve discomfort from others, inappropriately. For example, if you are unreasonably fearful of contamination from
chemicals, you may refrain from washing after deliberately
handling bottles of household cleaning products in a grocery
store. But if you allow yourself to wash several hours later
because you used charcoal lighter fluid to light coals in the
grill, you may still feel that the later washing removed the
feelings of "contamination" from the earlier, less difficult
exposure. This may represent an unplanned kind of response
delay, but it may also interfere with the process of habituation
to discomfort provoked by cans of household chemicals. One
solution is to reexpose yourself to the original circumstance
immediately after ritualizing, so that habituation can continue to the earlier exposure items. That is, after lighting the
grill and washing your hands, you must immediately handle
household cleaners.

Stopping Rituals "Cold Turkey"

Some treatment programs have asked patients to stop their
rituals altogether from almost the first day of formal exposure. There has been considerable variation in the strict-

ness of these programs. For example, researchers in London allowed their patients with washing rituals to continue "normal washing," meaning a few brief handwashings per day and a short daily shower. These washings—considered typical of non-obsessive behavior—were allowed throughout treatment, but patients were *not* allowed to wash after exposure to any items on their hierarchy. This method of exposure and ritual prevention produced good results in about 65 percent of the cases. It was considerably less strict than the blocking method of Victor Meyer and his associates, who conducted the first study of exposure and ritual prevention.

Meyer's group actually turned off the water to the faucets in the patients' rooms, and asked nurses to accompany them to the bathroom to make sure that no one washed when they weren't supposed to. The patients had to adhere very strictly to the no washing rules and were not allowed to carry out even "normal" washing. The group's results were excellent, with two-thirds of their patients much improved, and the remainder at least moderately improved.

Few treatment programs have been willing to restrict patients as severely as Meyer's did, but the outcome is worth remembering. It seems that stopping rituals completely from the beginning is very effective. It's true that Meyer used this method in an inpatient hospital treatment program; it may not be practical for those visiting therapists as outpatients, or trying to reduce fear and control rituals on their own. In the world outside a hospital, it may be difficult to prevent all access to water or have someone accompany you to the bathroom, and it may create real problems to go a week without bathing! But again, the outcome suggests that stricter ritual control is more effective treatment than gradual control—if you have the stomach for it.

Modified "Cold Turkey"

A compromise position on ritual prevention has been used by researchers in Philadelphia and in other places, including our own program in Boston. In this method, people with OCD are asked to stop their compulsions as completely as possible from the beginning of treatment. Sometimes it is impossible to avoid situations high on the hierarchy before you are ready to begin formal exposure to them. In this case, some exception to the requirement of *no* rituals may be made. But rules are established from the beginning to cover such circumstances: you must immediately reexpose yourself to feared situations that have already been confronted. That lets habituation continue for the lower items on your hierarchy; otherwise the ritualizing might relieve discomfort from the lower items as well as the higher items.

This program allows people with washing rituals to shower once every three to five days for a maximum of 10 minutes. It does not permit any handwashing except in situations in which dirty hands (for instance, from grease or ink) make it impossible to touch other things, shake hands, etc., without causing a visible problem. People with checking rituals are not allowed to check at all unless it is absolutely required by the situation (for example, a security guard's rounds), and those with repeating rituals are not allowed to repeat any action. This method has proved both manageable and effective in our treatment of OCD patients. The sections below focus on this modified cold turkey method, and offer more detail to help you plan for ritual prevention in conjunction with prolonged exposure to feared situations. You'll be able to modify its strictness if another program seems more appropriate to you—stricter or more lenient—but it's a good idea to begin by adhering to this program as described.

Managing Anxiety During Ritual Prevention

Chapter 7 suggested several strategies for coping with obsessive fears that provoke high levels of discomfort, especially when rituals are not allowed at all. These methods include logical self-talk to correct tendencies to catastrophize, the use of deep muscle relaxation, paradoxical exaggeration of fears, and humor. It is inevitable that stopping rituals, especially "cold turkey," will provoke discomfort. Just keep one or several of the coping strategies in mind, though, and you'll begin to discover other effective ways of defusing your anxiety. Refer to Chapter 7 for a detailed discussion of how to select and employ the coping methods best for you.

How To Carry Out Your Own Ritual Prevention

Planning Ritual Prevention

In the process of planning direct or imagined exposure to your obsessively feared situations, you must also plan carefully how to restrict your compulsive behavior. It is one thing to know you need to stop your compulsions, and quite another to successfully resist the urges to wash, check, or repeat in the midst of obsessive fear. Unless you have thought it through beforehand and made a clear plan, you are at great risk of giving in to these urges. In fact, you'll want to write the components of your plan down. This list will be an important part of treatment program.

Your best strategy is to think through what it will feel like to do each of the exposures that you have planned. Try to figure out what urges to ritualize you are likely to have following each exposure. Some people have more than one ritual they might turn to in a given situation. For example, when one man used a public restroom (sink, toilet seat, floor, door handle, etc.), he could 1) wash his hands, 2) merely rinse them if there was no soap, 3) use a "handiwipe" that he carried with him, 4) wipe his hands with alcohol, 5) brush his hands off, or, if all else failed, 6) he could think a "clean" thought about soap. He had developed a variety of creative but compulsive ways to make himself feel more comfortable following contamination, even in the most difficult of circumstances. Planning ahead in his case meant that he had to discard his handiwipes, avoid bringing or using soap, alcohol, or water, and perhaps put his hands into his pockets after exposure to contaminants to prevent himself from brushing them off. In addition, he would need to prevent himself from reducing anxiety by using mental rituals, which will be discussed further shortly.

Another man had obsessive fears of harm to his house or family from fire or burglary, as well as concerns about his car breaking down, about becoming ill or poisoned, about making mistakes, and about having bad luck from the number 13. He had a variety of checking rituals to reduce his fears about these obsessive concerns. In treatment, he had to plan carefully to avoid doing rituals that had become so habitual he no longer thought consciously about them. For example, he was aware that he took a long time to get from the garage into the house after parking the car, but could not really say exactly what he did that took so much time. In the planning stage, he asked his wife to watch him closely from a distance, to see what she observed; he himself kept a notebook of what he recalled checking. They used this strategy in several other situations where he tended to be slower than other people, especially in the bathroom in the morning, when leaving the house, and when getting out of the car. Together, their observations provided a detailed list of brief but persistent ritualistic acts of checking.

He and the therapist then planned exposures to progressively eliminate this compulsive checking in various everyday situations. Since concerns about the garage were the least disturbing, he planned ways of getting out of the car that would physically prevent him from checking. For example, he opened the car door and stepped out facing the house door, which he kept his eyes firmly fixed on until he had entered the house and closed the door behind him. In this way he was exposed to the garage, which triggered obsessive fears, but was not allowed to check repeatedly. Next, he eliminated his pre-bedtime ritual of checking the back door (which was never used), and rechecking the garage door (which he had already checked once on closing it), the stove, other kitchen appliances, etc. To prevent this checking, he would not let himself go into the kitchen or the garage before bed. If he really needed something in the kitchen, he went in without turning on the light, so it was too dark to check if he had an urge to do so. He planned and successfully learned to drink from glasses without holding them up to the light to look for spots; to drink milk and eat other foods without checking the label on the package; and to take his pills without saying the color aloud, reading the tiny label on the pill itself, or feeling the inside of his mouth with his tongue to make sure the pill was really there when he popped it into his mouth. Each exposure without checking required a pre-planned method of preventing himself from automatically carrying out his compulsions.

Guidelines for Ritual Prevention

In the course of conducting therapy with many people with OCD, we have developed some general guidelines which might help you decide how much to limit your compulsive behaviors. Most (although not all) people with OCD are concerned about situations that have some element of danger in them—a risk that might cause most people some concern, but that in the mind of the OCD sufferer becomes exaggerated in probability or degree. Similarly, compulsive actions are usually exaggerations of ordinary behaviors: everyone does some washing of themselves and their personal belongings; all people check some things they tend to forget or that can be dangerous if left untended. But what is "normal" behavior with respect to washing and checking? Those whose symptoms began later—in adulthood—have some personal perspective on what they *used* to do before they developed OCD symptoms. But others whose rituals developed during childhood or adolescence may have trouble understanding what is "normal."

For the purpose of treating OCD we define "normal" rather strictly, since changing ritualistic behavior requires a goal toward which you can strive. Normal washing can be considered one 10-minute shower per day (possibly a few minutes longer if a person does something extra like washing hair, applying a rinse, or shaving), and five or six handwashings per day. Obviously the number of handwashings will vary depending on what you do. Most people just wash their hands after using the toilet, getting their hands visibly dirty or greasy, or before eating a meal. Take these situations as your starting guidelines. On the other hand, doctors generally wash their hands after every patient they examine. Exceed the normal guidelines only if colleagues or peers do the same.

Normal checking for most people hardly ever means more than once, even when the situation is quite important, or even dangerous. Many people check a few things before leaving the house or going to bed: door locks, lights left on, appliances recently used, or small children in bed. People commonly check calculations (in the checkbook, for example) once to verify accuracy. They may check once to be sure they did something easily forgotten ("Did I remember to take my pills?"; "I can't recall if I left the check for the papergirl on the porch"). Normally, the situations checked are ones the person can't really remember clearly or can't control well (for example, because children might have been careless with an appliance) and where there is a reasonable likelihood of harm if it isn't taken care of. As a guideline for the person with checking rituals, it's best if nearly all checking is eliminated except that which family members or friends agree to be *essential*.

A few people repeat actions a certain number of times to ward off bad luck. If this is your problem, strive to stop it altogether; there is really no good reason to continue, no "normal" level of such behavior.

With respect to hoarding or saving rituals, many non-obsessive people do save things they may or may not eventually use, or collect objects merely as a hobby or memento of some occasion. In most such normal cases, however, the person has a clear attachment or fondness for the object or has a planned use for it. Furthermore, the saved objects don't take up household space needed for essential storage or for living. Keeping things without a clear and realistic plan for their storage and use is characteristic of compulsive hoarding. Ritual prevention would require you to throw out objects saved under these circumstances.

As suggested in Chapter 2, another form of ritual may be requests for reassurance. Reassurance may be sought from doctors about health issues, or from family or friends that some situation is safe or that something has been done properly. Asking for reassurance is a common act, but it is normally done no more than once, and usually only when the person asking is genuinely confused about something. One rule, then, is not to ask for verification or reassurance more than once. A second rule is not to ask a question you could answer for yourself. It is better to learn to use your own judgment, becoming more self-reliant despite uncertainty, than to depend on others' opinions.

It is easier to control requests for reassurance if those you turn to learn not to answer. Take time to remind them of the types of obsessive questions you put to them, and encourage them to hold back reassurance. They might say something like "I'm sorry, but I shouldn't answer that type of question for you." You can do this even with a professional such as your doctor, who may automatically answer your compulsive questions in a misguided effort to be supportive. In one situation, a woman who frequently called the "Poison Control" hotline about her children asked the hotline personnel to agree not to answer her requests for reassurance. This may be very difficult at first, for you and for them. But each time they answer a compulsive question, they have helped you ritualize and prevented you from exposing yourself effectively to your feared obsession. It's like being the "helper" of an alcoholic—not really a helpful thing at all if it perpetuates the illness!

In general, when using ritual prevention rules, it is better to err on the side of permitting too little than too much ritualizing. Whenever there is any doubt about whether a check or a wash is really necessary, *eliminate* it. You can always decide to wash more later, when your discomfort about contamination has eased, and you are guided more by reason than your wish to be less anxious. The stricter your program for treatment, the more probable that you will succeed in relieving your obsessive fears.

Note here that it is easier to change your compulsive behavior than your obsessive thinking. The suggestions in this chapter may seem daunting at first, but it's likely to require less of an effort to get your rituals under control, at least initially, than to decrease your fears through exposure. That doesn't mean you should fear exposure more. The latter will simply take longer; you must be patient. Tolerate and resist your urges to do compulsive actions and you'll find that the anxiety will subside on its own. Habituation makes your job easier: slowly the urges to ritualize will subside along with the anxiety, and ritualizing will become even easier to resist.

Blocking Mental Compulsions

Cognitive rituals can be more difficult to eliminate since they are not overt behaviors that you can simply decide to do or not to do. Like obsessive thoughts, they don't seem to be under voluntary control. Otherwise, you would just stop thinking upsetting things and OCD would not exist. Mental compulsions typically include prayers, thoughts, or images repeated in particular patterns (such as "good" thoughts to cancel "bad" ones), as well as numbers, songs, sayings, or phrases. These are usually repeated silently to offset some specific unpleasant idea or feared event. Often they can become so intertwined with the obsessively feared idea that it is hard to see where the obsessive (fear-increasing) idea ends and the compulsive (fear-reducing) idea begins. But as noted before, it is very important to separate the obsessive thoughts from the compulsive ones, since exposure is needed for one and ritual prevention for the other.

You will need some creativity to figure out how to block your own mental compulsions. The suggestions that follow offer some guidance. For those who find themselves saying "good things" (numbers, images, etc.) to offset bad ones, try blocking the ritual by deliberately thinking the very "bad" thought you are trying to avoid. For example, if you think the number 10 to neutralize your fear when the number 13 occurs to you, then immediately convert 10 back to 13 in your mind or say it aloud. If an image of loved ones in an auto accident leads you to try to imagine them safe and sound, immediately go back to the image of the accident and hold it as long as possible, at least until anxiety reduces somewhat. The idea is to end with the uncomfortable idea, much like going back to holding cans of chemicals after washing. That lets habituation, and not ritualization, ease your anxiety.

Besides the above method of returning your thoughts to the obsessive fear, another strategy for disrupting cognitive rituals is to distract yourself. Make it difficult—even impossible—to complete the ritual. You can distract yourself in any number of ways: singing a song, reciting something from memory, remembering something meaningful to you. You might also distract yourself with logical argument about why you don't need to do the ritual, reminding yourself at each step of what you are doing in treatment and why. Distracting yourself from ritualizing is very different from distracting yourself during exposure. Be sure to keep the distinction in mind: it can be useful to distract yourself from ritualizing, but you want to pay full attention to an exposure.

Another strategy of blocking mental compulsions is called thought-stopping. It consists of saying, first aloud and later silently, the word "Stop!" This ought to startle you and interrupt the cognitive ritual. The loud, harsh command can be considered a distraction method, or even a punishment for the ritual. Other punishments include snapping a rubber band against your wrist to produce a mild stinging, or simply pinching yourself. The pain then becomes associated with the ritual, and might help to reduce the urge to ritualize on future occasions.

Remember that each of these methods must be applied *only* to the mental ritual and *not* to the obsession. The obsession must be treated via exposure (such as holding the number 13 in your head, or the image of Jesus Christ's penis). Recently, one researcher described the use of tape-recorded sequences in which the person with OCD makes an endless loop tape of his own voice describing the anxiety-provoking obsession. The ritual is omitted from the tape, so that the patient can be exposed only to the obsession without interruption from ritualistic thoughts. The tape is played over and over again. This method appeared to work well in several cases, but has not yet been tested in a clinically controlled setting.

Summary

This chapter has described methods for stopping both behavioral compulsions and mental rituals. Ritual prevention should be carried out *simultaneously with exposure treatments.* That way obsessive fears are allowed to habituate without interruption from compulsions. Since compulsions often become habits with time, requiring little conscious thought, it is essential to plan how to block such behavior or thinking patterns in advance of exposure. Rituals can be delayed, gradually reduced in time, or prevented completely in easier situations first, followed by more difficult ones. Or they can be stopped altogether from the beginning of the exposure treatment. Stricter forms of ritual prevention appear to be the most effective. Ritual prevention must be planned carefully alongside the exposure program. Rules for "normal" behavior should be established so that you have specific guidelines to follow during treatment. Mental rituals require greater creativity to stop but must be prevented, just as overt rituals. Strategies such as returning to obsessive thoughts, distraction, and thought-stopping may help.

10

Should You Take Medications?

A simple answer to the question posed by this chapter title might be: yes, if they help. A more complicated (and more accurate) answer would be: yes, if the help they bring outweighs their side effects for *you*. But both of these answers may seem to beg the question, because what you really want to know is how much they will help—or hurt—*before* you try them. Unfortunately, this is just about impossible to predict accurately. The basic principle of trial-and-error, guided by some educated guesswork, is probably the only realistic option at this point in medical knowledge.

Because different people, even with the same symptoms, may react quite differently to the same medication, only first-hand experience can really give you the answers you need. This may imply that you should at least *try* a likely medication to see how it affects you before you judge whether medication treatment is for you. But there are other ways to look at it as well.

Some people argue that you should take medication only if you can't get the same help by other ways. This suggests that the other ways are somehow inherently better. A similar attitude is implied by people who describe medication for mental illness as "a crutch." But crutches are useful for people who need them, and some people need them all their lives; there is nothing shameful about needing to use a crutch. Obsessive Compulsive Disorder (OCD) may be as "physical" an illness as multiple sclerosis, even to the point of being associated with physical changes in the structure and function of the brain (see Chapter 3).

There is little doubt that certain medications can reduce obsessive-compulsive symptoms. Well designed research has repeatedly demonstrated this. But medications don't help everyone—typically, an effective antiobsessive medication helps only slightly more than half the OCD sufferers who take it. Even those who benefit from medication may get only partial symptom reduction.

These medications are not particularly toxic drugs—nothing like the drugs used for cancer chemotherapy for example—and their side effects are usually no more than annoyances. What's more, side effects often decrease to minor levels after a few weeks of continued treatment, and always cease after stopping medication.

One caution is in order about pharmacotherapy (medication treatment) for OCD: any beneficial effects, like the side effects, may not long outlast your use of the medication. There does seem to be a high risk of relapse following medication discontinuation. One study showed 90 percent of those who had benefited from clomipramine had relapses within a couple of months after stopping the medication. Behavioral techniques may help reduce this risk of relapse, but this remains to be proven. It is also possible that gains made with behavior therapy, while symptoms are reduced with drugs, may be lost when the drugs are withdrawn and the person has to face the full force of the obsessive fears.

Since OCD is typically a long-term or even lifelong condition, reliance on medication may mean indefinite medication treatment. This is not necessarily terrible. Many illnesses (hypertension, diabetes, etc.) require lifelong use of medication. Researchers don't know of any long-term ill effects from the antidepressant medications used to treat OCD; on the other hand, clinical experience with them goes back only about three decades, and perhaps longer term ill-effects remain to be discovered. In any case, lifelong treatment with a medication is nothing to be undertaken lightly.

Before you worry about what your decision in such a matter might be, remember that you'd only face the decision to take lifelong medication if you had already benefited substantially from it. Once you have been fortunate enough to gain a great deal from pharmacotherapy, your whole perspective on risks and benefits may become quite different. Some people who greatly fear a medication before trying it later become reluctant to stop it even when the doctor tells them to!

Many people with emotional problems "self-medicate" with alcohol or other drugs that are easy to abuse. These are generally much worse for you than anything a doctor is likely to prescribe. Most of the medications so far shown effective for OCD are available by prescription only, and do not pose any real risk of abuse or dependence.

Medication treatment is not really a "self-help" technique; you need a doctor's help with pharmacotherapy. But knowing something about medications can help you cooperate with your doctor in using the medication in the most effective way. Knowledge can also help you find the right doctor.

Finding the Right Doctor

As a person with OCD, your best bet is to seek medication treatment from a psychiatrist. Non-psychiatric physicians, such as general practitioners or internists, commonly prescribe psychiatric medications for well-known problems such as depression and anxiety. But general physicians are often unfamiliar with the *nature* of OCD itself.

Even some psychiatrists may be unfamiliar with this disorder. The OCD Foundation (P.O. Box 9573, New Haven, Connecticut 06535) may be able to help you locate a psychiatrist in your area who specializes in treating OCD. Or you might call the offices of the psychiatric association of your state for a list of such specialists. But psychiatrists who really specialize in treating OCD are few; many such specialists may be more interested in conducting research than treatment.

If you cannot locate a specialist in OCD, you might look for a psychiatrist who specializes in medication treatment of mental illness—sometimes referred to as a *psychopharmacologist*. Do not assume that all psychiatrists will be expert in using medications; some will have their main interest in psychotherapy or other forms of treatment which have not been proven helpful for OCD. If you do find a psychopharmacologist, bear in mind that such a person is *not* likely to also practice behavior therapy—which you probably need as well—and may not even know much about it or where to refer you. In that case, it will be up to you to find your own behavior therapist, as discussed in Chapter 6.

In working with your doctor to decide what medication to try, it will help you to know something about the scientific basis for considering medications effective. To do this you need to understand some basic facts about clinical research—research conducted on patients suffering from OCD. If you have the opportunity, consider taking part in such research as a subject yourself. You will be contributing to the improvement of knowledge about medication treatment for OCD, and perhaps getting help for yourself in the process. Clinical research projects can be a rewarding experience in mutual help for both researchers and patients.

How Medications Are Tested

The current standard for research on therapeutic drugs is the parallel-treatment, random-assignment, double-blind, placebo-controlled trial. What this complex phrase means is understandable if you take it apart.

Parallel treatment means that at least two treatments are compared "in parallel": they take place at the same time with two similar groups of patients. One group receives a certain treatment (A), while the other receives another treatment (B). It is important that the two groups be equivalent in all respects which might have a bearing on treatment results. For example, a patient who has been ill for years has the typical chronic form of OCD and may respond differently from the patient whose illness started only weeks or months before. The latter patient has an "acute" illness that just might clear up quickly and completely *without* treatment, although in OCD this is quite uncommon. Nevertheless, a disproportionate number of acutely ill patients in one treatment group as compared to the other would tend to bias the results.

To make sure that patients assigned to treatments A and B are similar, assignment of a given patient to a given treatment is usually done by a *random-assignment* process akin to flipping a coin. Even after such a procedure, it is usual to check at the end of the study to make sure that patients in the two treatment groups were similar in certain basic respects, such as how severely ill they were and how long they had been ill before coming for treatment.

Double-blind means that both the patient *and* the doctor are "blind" to whether treatment A or B is the one assigned to a given person. This is accomplished by having different medications packaged in identical capsules and bottles identified only by code numbers. No one directly involved with the treatment knows which code number is associated with which drug until the study is finished. Then the blind is "broken" by consulting a list matching codes and drugs. Of course, sometimes the telltale side effects of a certain drug will "break the blind" during the course of treatment, making it clear that the patient is receiving at least an active drug, rather than a placebo.

The procedure of blinding is intended to reduce the effects of the expectations and biases of both the doctor and the patient. For example, one or both may believe so strongly in the effectiveness of a certain treatment that they will perceive it to be working even when it isn't. Or it may *actually* work, but only through the power of suggestion (placebo effect) rather than through direct effects of the drug on brain biochemistry (pharmacological effect). The emphasis on blinding to combat bias reflects a respect for the powerful effects expectations can have on results.

To measure the placebo effect, one of the parallel treatments used in a study is often pharmacologically *inactive* as a drug—a "sugar pill," or a capsule without active ingredients. Such a study represents a *placebo-controlled* trial. In OCD, placebo effects are typically quite low—on the order of 10 percent. (By contrast, 30 to 40 percent of people with depression as their main problem will get better on placebo.) Sometimes the comparison treatment is not a placebo, but another active drug. Sometimes three treatments are compared—two active drugs and one placebo. Sometimes different dose levels of the same drug are compared with placebo. In most cases, a blind is easier to maintain when two active drugs or two doses of one active drug are compared than when an active drug is compared only with a placebo. For this reason, the positive results of studies showing one active drug to be better than *another* active drug are more impressive than results from studies that compare a drug only with a placebo.

Despite the best research design, a single study may, by sheer chance, give an incorrect and misleading positive or negative result. To guard against such chance findings, at least a few studies are generally necessary to establish a treatment as effective. If these few early studies produce conflicting results, several more studies may be necessary to resolve the disagreements. In the field of depression research, there are thousands of placebo-controlled studies; in the area of OCD, there are only dozens of studies, a comparatively small base of data to guide treatment choices. The problem is that *most* psychiatric drugs have either not received any controlled study in OCD, or not enough study to know whether they really work for OCD. Nevertheless, the results of studies with a *few* drugs are consistent enough to make some findings likely to be facts.

Which Medications Are Effective for OCD?

Clomipramine. One drug has received by far the most research attention. Clomipramine (brand name: Anafranil) has been available around most of the world (except the United States) for decades. It has been tested in almost a dozen different placebo-controlled studies in OCD; all have been positive. That is, all have shown clomipramine-treated patients doing better, with more improvement in obsessive-compulsive symptoms by the end of the study, than placebo-treated patients. Most of these studies were small, involving at most 20 to 40 patients, but the most recent trial involved hundreds of subjects. This "multicenter" study compared clomipramine only with a placebo, and clomipramine does have many side effects which might "break the blind" in comparing it with a placebo. What makes the research literature on clomipramine more impressive is that several controlled studies have compared it with chemically related "tricyclic antidepressants"—which include drugs like imipramine (Tofranil); amitriptyline (Elavil); etc.—having similar side effects. Most of these studies have found clomipramine more effective for OCD than the comparison drug. An impressive finding.

Why should clomipramine work better for OCD than other drugs to which it is closely related? There is actually a difference of only one chlorine atom between the otherwise identical molecules of clomipramine and imipramine. Imipramine is an effective antidepressant, according to many studies in depression, but it failed to do better than placebo in one study of OCD patients and did worse than clomipramine in another study. Yet another closely related and effective antidepressant, desipramine, did worse than clomipramine in all three studies where the two drugs were compared for OCD.

The "Serotonin Hypothesis" of OCD. Researchers have speculated that the special effectiveness of clomipramine in OCD depends on its special effects on serotonin, a specific neurotransmitter, or brain hormone. Imipramine also affects serotonin, but less so than clomipramine. Of the entire group of tricyclic antidepressants, clomipramine has the strongest effects on serotonin. Specifically, clomipramine inhibits the ability of the nerve cell to reabsorb (or reuptake) the serotonin it has secreted. Nerve cells secrete serotonin—and other neurotransmitters—in order to communicate with each other: chemicals such as serotonin transmit messages from one nerve cell to the next. Once serotonin is reabsorbed by a nerve cell, it becomes inactive until it is released again. If the serotonin *can't* be reabsorbed quickly (as results from clomipramine), serotonin activity is prolonged. This is thought by some to be what makes it helpful for OCD.

It is tempting to jump to the conclusion that since increasing serotonin activity helps OCD, OCD patients are somehow deficient in serotonin. However, this would be a misleading oversimplification. In the nervous system, any change made by an outside agent (like a drug) tends to be counteracted by opposite changes in the nervous system itself. This is called *homeostasis*, or the tendency of the nervous system to keep trying to regain its former state and thereby maintain its stability. It can do this, for example, by reducing sensitivity of receptors for the neurotransmitter (down-regulation) when activity of the neurotransmitter is increased by a drug. So, what at first seems to be a drug-induced *increase* in serotonin may end up having *opposite* effects further down the line.

All that a serotonin hypothesis of OCD can really say at this point is that there seems to be "something wrong" with serotonin in OCD patients, and that jolting the serotonin balance in these patients may be helpful to the nervous system in establishing a better equilibrium.

For a long time clomipramine was the most powerful *serotonin reuptake inhibitor* available. This is no longer the case, and newer drugs with "serotonergic" effects are attracting increasing attention for the treatment of OCD.

Newer Serotonin Reuptake Inhibitors. A few newly developed antidepressant drugs, not in the chemical family of tricyclics, appear to be still more powerful and selective in their effects on serotonin than clomipramine. By being more selective, they have fewer effects on other systems in the body and therefore have fewer side effects. These drugs have become a focus of much research interest in OCD. They have not been around as long as clomipramine and so have been subject to less study, but this situation is changing as more research is conducted.

The newer serotonin reuptake inhibitors include several drugs, some of which may be unfamiliar to you and one of which has received a lot of publicity. The lesser known drugs include fluvoxamine and sertraline; they are not yet available in the American market. But fluoxetine (brandname: Prozac) is available and has become well known. Calling Prozac by its brand name may help avoid confusion with fluvoxamine, which sounds similar to fluoxetine, but is chemically quite different.

Fluvoxamine and Sertraline. Of these newer serotonin uptake inhibitors, fluvoxamine has had the most study of its use on people with OCD, and may well become the second drug (after clomipramine) to get FDA approval for the treatment of OCD. A number of placebo-controlled studies have all shown it to be more effective, and another study has shown it more effective for OCD than the active comparison drug, desipramine. These results suggest that researchers are on the right track in looking at other serotonin uptake inhibitors besides clomipramine as promising treatments for OCD. Early results from a small study of sertraline have also been encouraging, and a larger study is underway. These drugs won't be discussed further here because of their relative unavailability right now, but you might gain access to them through research programs. Do consider trying treatment through this avenue if it is available to you.

Prozac. Since Prozac is freely available and well publicized, it is of special interest. Unfortunately, it was originally studied and marketed only as a treatment for depression. Little research has been done to test Prozac for OCD. It has been tried in a few "open" (not blind) and "uncontrolled" (no parallel treatment for comparison) studies. These results were encouraging, but are not yet enough to prove the drug effective for OCD. One double-blind, placebo-controlled study actually *failed* to show Prozac working significantly better than placebo, but the design of this study was seriously flawed and the results have to be taken with reservations. The pharmaceutical company that makes Prozac has started a large placebo-controlled study which should soon determine more clearly whether Prozac works for OCD. Meanwhile, many OCD patients will undoubtedly try it; early clinical experience does suggest it may work quite well, and perhaps with fewer side effects than clomipramine. At the same time, it's a good idea to remain skeptical of publicity that presents Prozac as a "miracle drug" or a panacea for all ills. It has actually never been shown more effective than any other active drug for any condition, including depression.

Which Medications To Try?

Clomipramine and fluvoxamine are better established than Prozac as effective antiobsessive treatments. However, Fluvoxamine remains unavailable in many countries, including the United States, where even clomipramine has only recently become available. Clomipramine, the only drug so far FDA-approved for the treatment of OCD, will generally be your first choice. When and if fluvoxamine is approved by the FDA for marketing in this country, it may have advantages in terms of less side effects.

Prozac is a drug that has enjoyed astounding popularity since its recent introduction to the American market. The drug has established a reputation for having few side effects, but publicity has created the illusion that it is a panacea. In fact, it has yet to be adequately proven effective for OCD. You may want to try Prozac if you have already tried clomipramine and failed to benefit or found the side effects hard to tolerate. Prozac, in general, will have fewer side effects, as will almost any newer antidepressant drug. The main thrust of drug development over the decades since clomipramine first became available has been to reduce side effects; by and large this effort has been successful, though not to the extent of eliminating all side effects. Some people may even find Prozac harder to tolerate than clomipramine. Remember, sucessful drug treatment is a highly individual matter.

What Are the Risks of Medication Treatment?

What should you expect in the way of side effects? This will obviously depend on which medication you take as well as how much you take of it. Clomipramine causes a wide range of side effects which are more nuisances than hazards: drowsiness, dizziness, faintness, dry mouth, constipation, blurred vision, rapid heartbeat, tremor, and nausea, among others. Most people who take an effective dosage of it will have one or more of these symptoms; few people will have all of them. These side effects tend to be most troublesome when you are just starting on the medication, or increasing the dose. Usually, they will gradually decrease and may even disappear completely over the course of weeks or months of taking the drug at a stable dose.

There is only a remote chance of dangerous side effects. An occasional person may become dizzy or faint enough to fall, potentially causing injury. Some may become so drowsy that they cannot drive safely. Common sense should prevent you from putting yourself at risk if you feel this way on a given drug. You may be at increased risk for dangerous driving by ingesting even small amounts of alcohol when you are also taking a sedative drug like clomipramine.

Clomipramine does seem capable of causing epileptic seizures slightly more often than other types of antidepressants; out of 1,000 patients treated with clomipramine, a few will have such a side effect. A seizure is dangerous, particularly if you are driving or operating hazardous machinery at the time. However, people with epilepsy survive seizures repeatedly during their lives. Virtually all antidepressants, even Prozac, have been occasionally associated with seizures without any other ill effects. In general, tricyclic antidepressants like clomipramine are not known to cause any life-threatening long-term effects, such as cancer, after decades of use in millions of people. Nor are they known to cause birth defects. On the other hand, these drugs have not been *adequately* studied in use during pregnancy, and should probably be avoided by women who are trying to become pregnant, or be stopped as soon as pregnancy occurs.

Clomipramine has a few effects on the functioning of the heart: it can increase the heart rate, while slowing the rate at which nerve impulses are conducted within the heart. However, these effects seem relevant only to people with specific types of preexisting heart disease, such as heart block.

The newer serotonin uptake inhibitors, like Prozac and fluvoxamine, are less prone than clomipramine to cause so-called "anticholinergic" side effects. The name anticholinergic derives from the belief that these side effects are caused by a blockage of nerve impulses transmitted by the neurotransmitter acetylcholine. Such side effects may include dry mouth, blurred vision, constipation, urinary hesitance, confusion, and memory impairment (although the last two are quite uncommon). Besides causing less anticholinergic effects, the newer drugs also cause less drowsiness, though an occasional person may become drowsy on Prozac. A decrease in blood pressure, sometimes associated with dizziness or faintness, is also less common with the newer drugs than with clomipramine. However, Prozac in particular seems to cause *overexcitement* and insomnia as side effects.

One area in which these newer drugs do cause problems for a substantial minority (perhaps a quarter to a third) of the patients who take them involves the gastrointestinal system. Indigestion, nausea, diarrhea, and sometimes even vomiting may occur. This can also happen with clomipramine.

With the newer drugs, you may notice a peculiar effect on sexual functioning—difficulty in achieving orgasm, despite becoming aroused and being able to participate in sex. This is called *anorgasmia*. It may occur with any of the serotonin reuptake inhibitor medications, including Prozac and clomipramine. Medications such as cyproheptadine (Periactin) or yohimbine (Yocon) may be tried to counteract this if it seems to be a serious problem. The main thing is to recognize anorgasmia as a reversible drug side effect rather than a permanent loss of sexual function.

Finally, some people will initially feel "wired" or over-stimulated—restless, fidgety, more nervous—in the first few weeks of treatment with these drugs, especially Prozac, and may at first feel they are getting worse, not better. If this becomes intolerable, to the point that you are tempted to stop taking the medication before giving it a "fair trial," you still have options. There are other medications that may be used temporarily to counteract these side effects, such as sleeping medications, antianxiety medications, or beta-blockers (such as propranolol, trade name: Inderal).

You may be worried about whether you will become "dependent" on the drug. If dependent means that you need the drug in order to feel relief from the symptoms of your illness, then the answer *might* be yes. Drug treatment for most psychiatric disorders seems to suppress symptoms, like aspirin for headaches, rather than cure the disease, like penicillin for pneumonia. Because OCD is typically chronic, its symptoms will commonly increase again after an effective drug is stopped, although this may take weeks or months to happen. On the other hand, you may have meanwhile found other ways, such as using behavioral techniques, to deal with them.

But if you are worried about a "dependency" that is like drug addiction, where over time you end up taking more and more of the drug and find that stopping it results in severe withdrawal symptoms with cravings to take more of it again, you have little cause for concern. A few people may build up some tolerance to these medications and need some increase in dosage, but hardly ever does anyone escalate doses to very high levels or abuse these medications. It is rarely a problem to stop taking them. The newer serotonin uptake inhibitors do not seem to cause withdrawal effects. Abrupt discontinuation of clomipramine may cause a "cholinergic rebound" withdrawal syndrome, characterized by nausea, diarrhea, and flu-like symptoms. But you can usually avoid this by gradually lowering the dosage ("tapering off") over the course of several days or a few weeks.

What Are the Benefits?

What can you expect in the way of benefits from a medication such as clomipramine? First of all, realize that not *everyone* with OCD is helped by this form of treatment. Even those who do benefit rarely experience a "cure." Rather, when the drug works, it is likely to reduce the frequency or intensity of your symptoms by some percentage, like 30 percent or 60 percent. You may obsess less often or feel less upset by obsessive thoughts. You may find it easier to resist compulsive urges. Obsessive-compulsive symptoms may occupy less of your day. Typical symptom improvement with effective antiobsessive drug treatment is on the order of 30 to 60 percent reduction from levels prior to treatment. This would probably be enough for you to feel that the medication made an important difference in your life, but not enough to make you feel really "well." You will probably then want to try other approaches, such as behavioral techniques, to progress further. Ultimately, those alternative approaches may allow you to get off medications without relapsing.

The "Fair Trial"

Once you start medication treatment, try to give it a "fair trial." It is unlikely to work overnight. It may not even *start* working for several weeks, and it may take several more weeks to show its full effects. At first, you may experience only side effects and no therapeutic benefits. This can be especially confusing if a drug like Prozac, with its stimulant-like effects, increases your anxiety temporarily. You may even feel that your illness is getting worse! But your doctor may be able to help by temporarily prescribing a counter-acting antianxiety medication such as alprazolam (brand name: Xanax), clonazepam (Klonopin), lorazepam (Ativan), or others. Propranolol (Inderal) is a different kind of medica-tion that might also help. Be cautious about taking too much of these antianxiety medications or using them for a long period of time, since you *can* become dependent on some of these drugs. They can also make you drowsy or unsteady. Still, you may find them very helpful for short-term use.

If you can only take a low dosage of clomipramine be-cause of its side effects, the treatment is less likely to work. On the other hand, if you give yourself time to "adapt" to the side effects, you may be able to tolerate higher doses as time goes on. A fair trial may require three months at a "full" dosage, which could be up to 250 milligrams per day of clomipramine. At first, you might have trouble handling even a single dose of 25 milligrams. The proper dosage of Prozac for best effects is still unclear. Some doctors think it works best at lower doses (such as a single 20 milligrams capsule per day), whereas others use it up to (and beyond) the maximum dosage recommended by the pharmaceutical company, 80 milligrams (four capsules per day).

Drug Alternatives

If you have given a medication like clomipramine or Prozac a fair trial and it still fails to give you the kind of benefits that most "medication responders" get, you may want to try another type. One alternative would be a different serotonin uptake inhibitor. For example, if you failed to benefit from clomipramine or found its side effects intolerable, you might want to try Prozac, or vice versa. Your doctor might choose to try "augmenting" or strengthening the effects of clomipramine or Prozac by adding to it another medication—such as lithium, buspirone (BuSpar), pimozide (Orap), fenfluramine (Pondimin), clonazepam (Klonopin), or others.

On the other hand, you might try drugs other than serotonin reuptake inhibitors. These may not have had much (or any) controlled study for the treatment of OCD, but may have been reported effective in individual cases. It is hard to evaluate the effectiveness of these drugs for OCD in a scientific way because each case report must be considered individually. Some early reports are more convincing than others.

One alternative is an antidepressant that mainly blocks serotonin receptors—trazodone (brand name: Desyrel). This is a sedative (drowsiness-producing) drug helpful against insomnia, and is sometimes combined with other antidepressants for this purpose.

Another alternative is the group of antidepressant medications called monoamine oxidase inhibitors (or MAOIs). These drugs are often avoided out of fear that they can cause dangerous rises in blood pressure when combined with the wrong foods (such as aged cheese) and other drugs. But they have proven extremely helpful for depression that does not respond to more standard antidepressant medications, and there are several reports of MAOIs helping OCD patients who have not responded to other drugs. In fact, almost all known psychiatric medications, and some medications not ordinarily considered psychiatric, have been tried and found helpful for one or another person with OCD. If you want to pursue different medications in an effort to get the most help for OCD this way, you will need to learn more about these other drugs than can be described in thse pages. A partial listing of relevant studies can be found at the end of this book. The material covered in this chapter may help make such scientific literature accessible and understandable to you.

Medication versus Behavior Therapy

Particularly if compulsive rituals are part of your OCD, try to take advantage of behavior therapy, not just medications. Rarely will you find a single therapist skilled in administering both, so you may have to go to two different treaters. Typically, you would consult a psychiatrist for medications and a psychologist, social worker, or nurse for behavior therapy. Of course, you may also be able to do much with behavioral techniques on your own, as described elsewhere in this book.

Some people will prefer to see what they can get out of behavior therapy alone at first. You may want to turn to medication only if behavior therapy doesn't work well enough. Or you may prefer to try medication alone at first. Medication can be easier to take than behavioral treatment, and sometimes it is enough. On the other hand, most OCD sufferers will find medication helpful, but not as much so as they would like. Then you might choose to pursue behavior therapy in an effort to make further progress.

Three specific types of OCD patients may find medication particularly important. First, if you are severely depressed, you may find yourself lacking the hope, energy, concentration, and will power to take advantage of behavioral techniques. Most of the drugs recommended here for OCD are also effective antidepressants. Even the commonly used tricyclic antidepressants, other than clomipramine, which do not seem so helpful for OCD itself, may be helpful for your depression if that is a big problem on top of your OCD.

Second, you may find medications especially important if you have only obsessive thoughts and no compulsive rituals. While there are behavioral techniques to treat the purely obsessive patient, they are not as well proven as the techniques of exposure and ritual prevention used to treat compulsive behaviors. Medications seem to work equally well for both obsessions and compulsions.

Finally, there are those people who, for various reasons, are not motivated enough for treatment to participate in behavior therapy. For example, a person may have lost insight into the unrealistic nature of his or her symptoms and may even start to defend them. Such a person might not be likely to read this book, but perhaps you are a relative or a friend of someone like this. In such cases, a medication may be accepted by the patient, whereas a complex and anxiety-provoking behavioral program may not. There is always the hope that medication treatment will alleviate OCD to the point where behavior therapy will become possible. We believe that behavior therapy is the first choice treatment whenever this is feasible—but it may not always be enough, it may not always be available, or it may not be acceptable to the OCD sufferer.

Summary

Medication is not a self-help technique; you need a doctor skilled in using medication to treat psychiatric disorders and as knowledgeable as possible about OCD. However, you can help yourself in finding and working with such a doctor by knowing more about medication treatment for OCD.

So far, only a couple of medications have been really proven effective for OCD —clomipramine and fluvoxamine —of which only clomipramine (Anafranil) is readily available in the United States at this time. However, another drug, Prozac, is available and similar enough in its serotonin effects —thought to be key to antiobsessive effects—to be worth trying in spite of its not yet being scientifically proven effective for OCD.

There are many pros and cons to medication, but you cannot really tell what a given drug will do for *you* in particular until you have given it a "fair trial" of adequate dosage and duration. The biggest drawback of drug treatment may be the need to continue the drug indefinitely to retain the effects. Behavior therapy may be preferable for this reason. But certain people—those who are most depressed, or who lack motivation for a behavioral program—may need medication as their mainstay. And partial improvement with medication may be important in helping "set the stage" for behavior therapy.

11

Other Strategies in the Treatment of OCD

So far, this book has focused on the two types of treatment demonstrated effective for Obsessive Compulsive Disorder (OCD): behavior therapy and medications. The assumption has been that readers will seek treatment on an outpatient basis, or undertake it entirely on their own, rather than in the hospital. But there are alternatives that someone with OCD might face at some point in his or her treatment. These include hospitalization, electroconvulsive therapy, psychotherapy, and psychosurgery.

Hospitalization

Many people with OCD are never hospitalized at all for psychiatric treatment. This stands in contrast to many of those with other mental disorders, such as schizophrenia, manic-depressive illness, and even depression. Such people are often treated as inpatients, even if their hospital stays are intermittent and brief.

Occasionally, OCD patients become so severely ill that they require hospitalization. They may have OCD symptoms within the context of another, more severe diagnosis such as schizophrenia or manic-depressive illness; or they may just have very severe OCD. Still, most people with OCD can become severely symptomatic without ever being hospitalized. Some educated guesswork can point to why this might be so.

Characteristically, OCD allows people to function to some extent, with a great deal of effort, in spite of symptoms. The OCD sufferer typically stays in contact with reality, even when obsessive-compulsive symptoms seem quite bizarre. OCD rarely leads to violent or self-destructive behavior; if anything, OCD sufferers tend to be inhibited rather than dramatic in their behavior. A person who is not psychotic, violent, or suicidal, and who is able to meet at least the minimum demands of life—or get someone else to meet them—can generally stay out of a mental hospital if he or she wants to. The tendency of OCD sufferers to feel embarrassed by or ashamed of their symptoms can make them very sensitive to the perceived stigma of mental hospitalization. Furthermore, the typical course of OCD—marked by chronicity or waxing and waning symptoms rather than by "episodes" of acute illness—does not lead to distinct periods of "being sick" that stand apart from the chronic condition. In other illnesses, such periods of drastically altered functioning provide one of the indications for hospitalization.

But there are specific circumstances that might make it necessary, or at least advantageous, for you to consider hospitalization. For one thing, at least a third of all OCD sufferers go through one or more periods of major depression at some time in their lives. Such major depressions may lead to incapacitation or thoughts of suicide, either of which ordinarily indicate a need for hospitalization. The hospital can provide relief from many of the demands of everyday life, increased support from others, and a measure of added safety.

Another reason why an OCD sufferer might benefit from inpatient treatment is the greater intensity of supervision that this setting allows. For example, in one study patients had the water turned off in their rooms and were escorted to the bathroom by nursing staff, to prevent excessive washing. Extreme as it may sound, this nevertheless worked very well. In an outpatient setting, it is rarely possible to have personal supervision by a behavior therapist for more than a few hours a week. Sometimes relatives may help extend the personal supervision at home, but often no one is around full time, and sometimes tensions with available relatives make it hard for them to help effectively. You may simply need a more supportive environment to help you begin to confront your fears. Of course, you will eventually need to confront those fears in the environment where you live, but that may become easier once you have started to deal with them in the hospital.

If the OCD sufferer has lost a substantial amount of insight into and resistance against his or her symptoms, the support of hospital staff may be all the more important. Behavior therapy in the hospital can be supplemented by "operant" techniques—reward and punishment—as well as the exposure with ritual prevention described in this book. A person who requires this kind of external control is not likely to rely on a book such as this; but perhaps you are a relative of a severe sufferer and would like to help. The hospital might be an invaluable ingredient of treatment in such cases.

Sometimes there are diagnostic questions that can be resolved by further testing—for example, whether a given set of symptoms really represents OCD, rather than some other illness such as temporal lobe epilepsy. It is often easier to coordinate multiple tests, examinations, and consultations in a hospital than out of it. Multiple mental and physical illness may coexist in the same person, making treatment quite complicated.

At times, the course of medication treatment may not flow smoothly. Side effects can persist, or problems can develop when one medication interacts with another or with physical illnesses. In such cases, administration of medications in the hospital is significantly safer than at home. Dosages and blood levels can be adjusted and checked more rapidly, and systems can be monitored that might be affected by medications, such as heart function and blood pressure.

Finally, there are pragmatic issues that you might not think relevant to the matter of hospitalization but that sometimes play a larger role than people are willing to admit. Specialized OCD treatment is often available only at specific centers, possibly far from where you live, and it may be impractical to commute from home to such a center. Also, for many people insurance coverage for outpatient mental health services is much more limited than for inpatient services. The intensive nature of supervised behavioral treatment may simply exceed your financial resources, unless you admit yourself to a hospital to take advantage of greater insurance benefits.

Many people may consider hospitalization unacceptable because of a perceived stigma, or because of interference with their work and family caretaking responsibilities. Usually hospitalization *can* be avoided. But when powerful factors such as those described above combine to make hospitalization indicated, and you still resist the idea, you might ask yourself whether you are in fact avoiding not so much the hospital as the steps necessary to deal effectively with your OCD. It's a tough question to think about. But your desire to get better may be offset by an understandable fear of the treatment process, now that you see what's involved. After all, effective treatment for OCD requires confronting your fears, which means *feeling* fear, at least for a while. But remember that only by confronting your fears will you free yourself of anxiety that might otherwise stretch ahead for a lifetime. A hospital setting can provide the intensive support you may need to take those first few steps.

Electroconvulsive Therapy

One form of treatment that is difficult to obtain in any other setting than a hospital is electroconvulsive therapy (ECT), also known as "shock treatment." This is indeed a shocking term to many people; it may call to your mind images from popular literature and movies that portray it as a form of medieval torture. This is a very unfortunate misconception.

ECT involves a "shock" in the sense of passing an electrical current across the head, sufficient to provoke a seizure, which is a brief period (seconds) of paroxysmal electrical activity in the brain. This is very much like the grand mal seizure an epileptic might have, except that during ECT the patient is anesthetized and given muscle relaxants so that nothing like a seizure is visible to an observer. Nor is the patient conscious of experiencing anything during the treatment itself. It is like going for surgery except that no scalpel is used and nothing is cut or sewn: you have an intravenous needle placed in a vein in your arm, a short-acting barbiturate flows through intravenously, you lose consciousness, and when you awaken a few minutes later it is over. The usual after-effects are some confusion and forgetfulness which can last minutes or hours, and possibly a headache. Some people notice hardly any after-effects at all, although generally after several treatments some (temporary) loss of memory will occur. A few people have claimed long-lasting memory impairment from ECT, but scientific studies have generally found memory to be *improved*, presumably as a result of improvement in depression.

ECT is an excellent treatment for severe depression, perhaps the best one known. In cases where depression has led to suicide attempts or loss of contact with reality, ECT may be essential and life-saving. Some OCD patients on occasion become this severely depressed; in such cases, they should not be deterred by the "bad press" of ECT from receiving what is really a very safe and effective treatment.

On the other hand, ECT is *not* usually part of the treatment for OCD patients. Even those prone to depression—unless it is especially severe—are more likely to be treated with antidepressant medications. ECT has actually received little study for the treatment of OCD. There are a few favorable case reports, although one larger study indicated that ECT was less effective in treating OCD than treatments with which it was compared. ECT probably deserves further study as a treatment for severe cases of OCD. If it really does not work well, this would provide further evidence that OCD differs from depression, which generally responds very well to ECT.

Psychotherapy

It may seem odd to you that only at this late stage of the book do we deal with psychotherapy. Psychotherapy is probably the treatment most familiar to you; it is often referred to just as "therapy," or as "counseling." Psychoanalytic (also known as psychodynamic) psychotherapy is the most common variety, but there are many others—Gestalt, interpersonal, etc. Psychotherapy of one sort or another has been part of the treatment histories of most obsessive-compulsive patients we see.

Naturally, the results of therapy for most of these people have been unsatisfactory; otherwise, they wouldn't go to the trouble of seeking out "OCD specialists" for help! It may be that there are many OCD patients who get better with the usual type of psychotherapy and never come to need behavior therapy, medications, or specialized consultations. If so, however, they are not much reported on by the psychotherapists who treat them.

One of five full case histories written up by Sigmund Freud—and the only successful case he directly treated—was a case of OCD, "the Rat Man," published in 1907. Many analysts today feel that this case represents a "transference cure"—the success of the power of suggestion and the wish of the patient to please the therapist. Nonetheless, the Rat Man recovered from his symptoms after Freudian psychoanalysis. In 1985, a researcher named Peter Sifneos reported good results in nine of 10 carefully selected OCD patients treated with his specific form of brief psychodynamic psychotherapy. However, these patients were carefully selected for treatment and may not have had typical cases of OCD, since each had a relatively recent and acute onset of symptoms. To our knowledge, there has never been a controlled study of psychodynamic psychotherapy for the treatment of OCD.

One problem with the psychoanalytic literature on OCD is that it often confuses OCD with obsessive-compulsive personality disorder (OCPD). Indeed, one psychoanalytic writer, Leon Salzman, proposes that OCD and OCPD really lie along a continuum, without any sharp dividing line between the two. Dr. Salzman agrees that OCD does not respond well to the traditional, long-term psychodynamic treatment in which a lot of time is spent discussing childhood and the distant past of the patient. But he argues that the best treatment for OCD—better even than behavior therapy—is a form of here-and-now therapy in which the therapist takes an active role and focuses on the person's current relationships, including the relationship with the therapist. Dr. Salzman emphasizes the need for obsessive-compulsive patients to learn to take risks in life, which has some parallel to the process of exposing oneself to feared situations. He also emphasizes accepting the limits of your ability to control events and to do things perfectly.

All this sounds like good advice. Whether it is effective in actually treating the symptoms of OCD remains to be seen. One of the pitfalls of entering conventional psychodynamic psychotherapy is that it tends to encourage talking about things, rather than doing them. This is the opposite of what an OCD patient needs from a behavioral perspective. Behaviorists argue that overemphasis on talk may offer the patient an "out" from actual exposure. After all, if you feel that just *talking* about your fears and compulsions—and the hypothetical reasons behind them—represents appropriate and adequate treatment, you might never get around to the much more difficult business of *exposing* yourself to feared situations and suppressing compulsive responses.

Another pitfall is that such traditional psychotherapy, contrary to behavior therapy and even to the therapies of Dr. Sifneos and Dr. Salzman, may go on interminably. You might remain in therapy for years without seeing any concrete impact on your OCD symptoms and without anyone coming to the conclusion that it just isn't working. OCD sufferers, in particular, seem to have a problem with getting "stuck" in situations and behaviors that aren't productive for them, including therapy (and medications) that don't work.

If this sounds like a disturbingly negative assessment of psychotherapy for OCD, bear in mind that this book is written by a behavior therapist (Dr. Steketee) and a psychopharmacologist (Dr. White). We are naturally prejudiced in favor of our own approaches. On the other hand, we both feel that psychotherapy can be helpful in certain other areas apart from obsessive-compulsive symptomatology—in understanding oneself better, in improving one's interpersonal relationships, in setting goals. For these reasons, many of our patients are involved in psychotherapy even while they undertake behavior therapy and pharmacotherapy for the more specific symptoms of their OCD. But we do suggest that during the most intensive parts of behavior therapy, patients postpone contact with other therapists to avoid receiving confusing or contradictory instructions regarding exposure and ritual prevention. Too many cooks can spoil the broth!

Psychosurgery

In contrast to the commonplace use of psychotherapy for OCD, the use of psychosurgery (neurological surgery for psychiatric disorders) is quite rare nowadays. Nonetheless, cases of OCD that have proven resistant to behavioral or medication treatments are still among the indications for this approach. As much as ECT suffers from "bad press," psychosurgery suffers even more so. You may share a common notion of the typical operation as a "lobotomy" which leaves the patient "like a zombie."

However, psychosurgery has changed a great deal since the 1930s and 1940s. The old procedure involved inserting a knife in the front part of the brain and cutting all connections between the frontal cortex and parts of the brain further back, causing a great deal of destruction to brain tissue in the process. These procedures had a significant mortality rate (2 to 4 percent), and not uncommonly led to complications such as epilepsy and undesirable personality changes. About half the OCD patients treated with this type of procedure improved, although often just to the extent of being less bothered by their obsessive-compulsive symptoms, and not to the extent of being free of them.

Newer psychosurgical procedures involve far fewer lesions to the brain, very rare mortality, fewer complications, and possibly better overall results. Names for specific procedures include: orbital undercutting, stereotactic tractotomy, anterior cingulotomy, bimedial leucotomy, and limbic leucotomy.

Because all neurosurgical procedures involve making changes in the brain that cannot be reversed (as opposed to drug effects, which almost always disappear after the drug is stopped), psychosurgery remains a treatment of last resort. It is an option for people who are tormented by symptoms that other treatments haven't helped. Someone very experienced in the treatment of OCD should determine whether alternative treatments have really been exhausted. Then both family and patient should study the latest results of specific procedures at whichever treatment centers are accessible to them. You will find that the centers that do these procedures can provide the most information about them.

At the Massachusetts General Hospital (MGH), for example, the procedure performed is the anterior cingulotomy. This treatment involves the implantation of minute radioactive seeds (Yttrium 90) in the brain which cause very limited areas of tissue destruction around them before they rapidly decay and lose their radioactivity. Mortality has been almost absent after operations on hundreds of patients, and intellectual functioning is generally improved, not impaired. Many treatment-resistant patients have benefited significantly. Still, experience at MGH has been more with cases of depression and manic-depressive illness than with Obsessive Compulsive Disorder. Acceptance for the procedure requires a thorough review of all prior treatment records and direct interviewing of the patient by a panel of MGH psychiatrists; this is itself a complex and lengthy process which assures that no one will undergo the procedure without a great deal of thought as to its necessity and appropriateness.

Psychosurgery, like electroconvulsive therapy, may be a life-saving procedure for those who really need it. It would be a mistake to dismiss it summarily on the basis of fear without real knowledge. But real knowledge of the pros and cons of specific psychosurgical techniques goes beyond the scope of this book, and will require specific consultations with those who practice these procedures or screen patients for them.

Summary

The usual treatment for OCD takes place on an outpatient basis and involves behavior therapy or medication, or a combination of the two. Still, there may be good reasons for periods of treatment in the hospital. These include severe depression or psychosis in an OCD patient; the need for more intensive behavioral supervision than is possible on an outpatient basis; diagnostic uncertainty requiring rapid coordination of multiple tests and consultations; co-occurring medical or mental illnesses or multiple medications requiring special supervision; the unavailability of expert treatment close to home; or the need to access better mental health benefits in order to afford adequate treatment. One alternative treatment not practiced outside the hospital is electroconvulsive treatment, which is appropriate only for the most severely depressed OCD patients.

Psychotherapy is much used but little studied for OCD. It may have much to offer in specific areas such as self-understanding and improvement in interpersonal relationships. However, it may have less to offer for specific symptoms of OCD. Psychotherapy can mislead you into avoiding confrontation with feared situations if you believe that just talking about such matters is sufficient.

Psychosurgery is a treatment of last resort, but one which should not be dismissed out of hand. Some unfortunate OCD sufferers may find relief in nothing else. Keep in mind that neurological procedures have changed greatly since the old days of "lobotomies" and now have very few ill effects. Furthermore, these procedures are surrounded by many safeguards to limit their use only to those who really need them.

12

How To Manage Complications

For most people with Obsessive Compulsive Disorder (OCD), behavioral treatment will result in considerable improvement in fear and rituals. It is rare, however, that people experience complete remission of all symptoms. Some continued struggle with obsessive thoughts and compulsive urges is inevitable. Because of this, it is very important to plan strategies for coping with anticipated and unanticipated complications after treatment. This chapter will discuss several types of complications that can occur during and after treatment for OCD. Some are specific to the treatment context, such as trouble getting motivated or the emergence of new types of obsessive fears or compulsive behaviors. Others pertain to your life circumstances, either personal or interpersonal. Some life situation problems seem to result directly from the OCD, whereas others appear to have arisen independently but have an impact on the treatment process.

People who come to our clinic for treatment for OCD almost always suffer from some additional type of psychological difficulty. Common problems include severe depression, social fears (often associated with unassertiveness), other phobias, panic attacks, and obsessive or compulsive personality traits. Alcohol or drug abuse may have developed as part of an effort at "self-medication." OCD symptoms may have interfered with schooling or employment, so that the normal phases of life development have been interrupted. Marital or relationship difficulties may complicate the picture. Often when a psychological problem has been present in one family member for a long period of time, interactions within the family become dysfunctional and family members cannot figure out how to resolve them.

This chapter will discuss the types of complications most often encountered, and suggest methods for managing them in the context of exposure and ritual prevention treatment.

Motivation and Compliance

As noted in Chapter 6, it takes great courage for a person with OCD to expose him- or herself to fearful situations, especially when this exposure involves giving up a primary method of coping with anxiety—compulsive rituals. The first decision you face is whether you're willing to try to get rid of your obsessive-compulsive symptoms. To make this choice, you must believe that the obsessions are unreasonable or unfounded fears and that the compulsions interfere substantially with normal everyday functioning. In fact, the OCD symptoms must be *so* unpleasant that treatment by exposure and ritual prevention seems more desirable than having to carry out the compulsions. For people with only mild symptoms that interfere minimally with their daily living, it may not seem worth the unpleasantness of exposure treatment;

such people may prefer simply to keep their brief compulsions. On the other hand, if the obsessions and rituals are mild, then exposure may not be difficult, only briefly or mildly disturbing. Since OCD tends to be a chronic and often worsening disorder, it is much better to confront fears early in the process, before they become debilitating. Early intervention allows people to develop more adaptive coping strategies for managing fear and compulsive urges.

A second problem of motivation may occur during the treatment process. When treating patients in our clinic, we find that once they have agreed to undergo the behavioral treatment, most are very honest about reporting their feelings and their mistakes— that is, rituals they did that they weren't supposed to do. With a therapist to report to frequently, you can usually correct problems in the way you are carrying out exposures or ritual prevention. Similarly, if you are conducting your own treatment, you can be honest with yourself about when you avoid exposure to a particular situation and when you permit a ritual that you know is not in your best interest. Occasional mistakes followed immediately by corrective action (reexposure or more strict ritual prevention) will not cause great problems.

It may be helpful for you to see some concrete examples of "bending" the rules. Occasionally people find themselves replacing the prohibited ritual with a less obvious avoidance pattern. For example, one woman found that using hand lotion "decontaminated" her almost as successfully as washing; she began to use lotion regularly before realizing the problem. Brushing off hands or blowing off "germs" may also substitute for washing. Although only minimally intrusive, these new rituals need to be prevented to allow you to learn that anxiety decreases even with *no* ritual of any kind. Another type of avoidance problem is the case of a man who put "contaminated" clothing back in the closet for a second wearing, but made certain that it did not touch "clean" garments. Another person waited to enter public restrooms until someone came out and thereby eliminated his need to touch the doorknob. "Forgetting" something that required a return to the kitchen allowed one woman to subtly recheck that the stove was off.

These substitute mini-compulsions reflect ambivalence about the need to get rid of *all* avoidance and rituals. They hinder habituation to obsessive fears by contributing to the erroneous belief that such avoidance actually protects you from harm. Whenever you find yourself cheating on a regular basis in treatment, it is far better to stop the program than to continue. Otherwise you may convince yourself that treatment doesn't work, when in fact you just haven't been getting the right treatment.

Exposure and ritual prevention will become an exercise in frustration if it is sometimes done strictly and sometimes the rules are bent. Excuses for bending the rules regularly or not following them altogether vary. Usually there is uncertainty about whether it is necessary to confront *all* of one's fears and give up *all* rituals. You may feel that some of your fears are well-grounded, although others clearly disagree; even in calm moments, you may believe some obsessions and rituals necessary to prevent actual catastrophes. Unless you can either convince yourself of the unreasonableness of all your OCD symptoms or take the risk that you are wrong in your assessment of certain obsessive situations, you will have trouble successfully completing a program of exposure and response prevention. In that case, your attitude about your fears must change before exposure treatment can work well. Unfortunately, little is known about how to change attitudes. What *is* known is that changes in behavior often lead to changes in attitude. In fact, it may be far more effective to *do* something different or risky than to try to convince yourself logically that it is safe.

Development of New Obsessions

In our years of clinical experience with OCD patients in treatment, we have observed several situations in which new fears appeared to develop when the older ones declined. These new fears were also obsessive in nature and were accompanied by urges to carry out rituals which were usually but not necessarily similar to pretreatment rituals. In some cases, it seemed that the "new" fears were really old ones which the person became more aware of when the current obsessions, confronted during exposure treatment, became less prominent. In one case, for example, a man was fearful of objects or people that came from a particular city because that was the site of a radioactive spill in a laboratory he had worked in. During treatment, as the fear of that city declined considerably, he became aware of fears that touching the laboratory animals he worked with would lead to skin disease and eventual disfigurement or physical incapacitation. He feared this would lead others to pity or avoid him. The new fears were related thematically to the original fears of disease (especially of the skin) from the radioactive spill, which had since been replaced by a fear of the city and its contents. In his case, as he confronted the "new" fears during exposure, his anxiety diminished and no new obsessions emerged.

In another case in which new obsessions appeared during treatment, the connection to the original fears was less apparent. One woman feared contact with dog, bird, or human feces, as well as dead animals, and washed excessively (up to three hours a day) to remove imagined contamination. She avoided a variety of things connected with these sources of fear, including garbage trucks, public restrooms, street gutters, car tires, and brown spots on the sidewalk. Exposure and ritual prevention substantially reduced these fears, but some general anxiety remained, and she often scanned her environment for possible sources of danger. A few weeks after exposure therapy ended, she found herself obsessively fearful of running over pedestrians on the street, especially when turning a corner or glancing in the mirror to change lanes. These fears persisted for several hours after each incident occurred. When she increased her driving and avoided looking in the mirror to check behind her, agreeing to stop the car only when she was 100 percent certain that she had really hit someone, her fears gradually decreased.

Possibly, the new obsession was related to the old contamination fear in that both situations caused concern about being a "bad person," either by being dirty or being careless of others' safety. She recalled a childhood memory of her mother saying that the eczema on her arms, legs, and face represented the "bad" part of her coming to the surface. This fear of being bad was reinforced by a strict religious upbringing in which God was viewed as very punitive. As an adolescent, she made a personal vow to be a "responsible person." The obsessive-compulsive behaviors of cleanliness and carefulness in driving were an effort to keep her vow.

Some people with OCD change obsessions and compulsions over time. In such cases, it is important to search for underlying themes that connect the fears, as discussed in Chapter 6. For example, fears of being wrong or making mistakes may lead to ritualistic attempts to be perfect, along with much indecision about what the "right" thing to do is; fears of being responsible for something bad happening may result in avoidance of all sorts of risk taking. As treatment progresses, those who have suffered from a variety of obsessive ideas, following themes such as these, may develop new ideas that need to be addressed in the same manner of exposure and ritual prevention. Eventually, as your underlying ideas begin to change or at least become more easily recognized and countered, new OCD problems will cease to occur.

Be prepared that in times of stress, obsessive fears are still likely to occur. In the past, your obsessive ideas were commonly associated with feelings of discomfort; when discomfort emerges now, in another context, the obsessive ideas may still seem associated. During stressful times, you may also have less extra energy; it becomes harder to continue behaving in the most sensible manner when you confront the sort of irrational ideas that occasionally occur to everyone.

Coexisting Psychological Disorders

Nearly everyone in our clinic who suffers from OCD also has an additional psychological diagnosis. This may not be true for those of you with milder symptoms, but it seems almost inevitable for those with more severe and chronic OCD. Sometimes the additional problems appear to result directly from the OCD symptoms, for example, depression or generalized anxiety. The obsessive and compulsive symptoms can be so pervasive and debilitating that you get depressed about your inability to do things you would like to do, like get out of the house or drive a car. When anxiety about the obsessive idea is very high, and obsessive fears follow a very general theme, such as risk taking or perfectionism, anxiety itself may become so generalized that you approach most situations with fear. Such problems with depression and anxiety often decrease as the OCD symptoms improve and therefore may not require additional help beyond the main treatment for OCD.

When obsessions and compulsions begin in childhood or early adolescence, they can interfere with your comfort in ordinary social interactions. We have seen problems with fear and avoidance of dating, inability to express anger, unassertiveness in getting one's needs met by family or friends, and excessive concern or embarrassment when talking to others. This may lead to an avoidance of most social situations, except perhaps those with the closest family members. In some cases, you may know what behavior would be most appropriate in social situations, but feel too fearful to do it. Or, in addition to being fearful, you may feel inept or unskilled at expressing yourself with others.

Obviously, if problems with social situations interfere significantly with your ability to live in a satisfying way, you will want to resolve them. Sometimes it is crucial to do work on these issues from the beginning of treatment, because the social fears prevent you from resolving the OCD symptoms. In other cases, social anxiety continues even after OCD problems have been resolved, preventing you from engaging in meaningful activities even after treatment ends. You may find it difficult to fill time once spent on obsessions and rituals with more adaptive life activities. But if you leave too much spare time unfilled, obsessions and compulsions are likely to intrude and become reestablished. We urge you to evaluate for yourself whether social fears or a lack of social skills are likely to cause problems during exposure treatment, or especially afterward. If so, consider consulting a professional for help in resolving them. Self-help and support groups—of fellow OCD sufferers or more generalized recovering patients—can also help you with this. To locate such groups in your area, contact the OCD Foundation at P.O. Box 9573, New Haven, Connecticut 06535.

Another complicating factor for some people can be a compulsive personality style. This may manifest itself in several ways: preoccupation with details, rules, order, or schedules so that the major point of an activity is lost; reluctance to allow others to do things for fear they won't do them correctly; perfectionism that interferes with completing tasks; excessive devotion to work to the exclusion of social life (the "workaholic"); indecisiveness; being overconscientious or inflexible about moral or ethical issues; lack of generosity even in small ways; and trouble expressing affection toward loved ones. Of course, many people have one or two of these traits that are no more than personal quirks, such as hating to be late to events or appointments. But if you find that several of these apply to you, you may have a more difficult time resolving related OCD symptoms.

For example, if you are preoccupied with details, you may have more trouble stopping checking rituals because of your belief that checking is another way to make sure your life is "in order," and that you have exercised proper care to avoid future problems. Similarly, you may save things, not for sentimental reasons, but in case someday you need them; you may have trouble recognizing that the saving has become a "hoarding" ritual to the point that saved objects occupy important living space. Only when the rituals really interfere with everyday activities might you agree, even then reluctantly, to seek help. It may require a fundamental shift in attitude about what is important in your life for you to significantly reduce your checking or saving. You may have to reassess your priorities: always having at hand everything you need and never having to repurchase anything, or having space and freedom in which to live more fully.

Relationship Problems

We have been impressed by how often our OCD patients report and demonstrate caring and positive relationships with spouses, unmarried partners, and other family members. In fact, a study we conducted indicated that clinic patients with OCD were *no less* happy with their marriages than the average population. This was a little bit surprising in view of the major burden that OCD symptoms place on the sufferer and his or her family! Apparently, most people are able to adjust to the adversity presented by such psychiatric symptoms.

Of course, not all couples or families have been able to adjust to a member's OCD symptoms. Frequent arguments, lack of communication, threats to leave, separation, and even divorce can seem to result directly from ritualistic behavior. It is difficult to advise people how to manage their relationships in the face of such problems, but here are a few suggestions which may apply to your situation.

Some angry, unpleasant, and inconvenient reactions to OCD symptoms are inevitable. These reactions need not be viewed as problems, so long as the anger is appropriate to the situation and is directed not at the OCD person's *character*, but at his or her *behavior*. However, frequent criticism is a potential problem area for many people with OCD. This may be especially true if you are socially fearful, since you are more sensitive to the negative emotional overtones accompanying critical comments. In general, clinic patients with OCD who lived with highly critical or frequently angry family members were more likely to relapse over time. Studies of patients with *other* types of psychiatric diagnoses found that frequent critical comments (made during a family interview) were associated with a tendency to drop out of treatment or relapse over time. These research findings, as well as our own impressions, suggest that the angrier family members feel and the more openly critical they are, the harder it will be for the OCD sufferer to apply the exposure and ritual prevention techniques and maintain a commitment to resisting urges to ritualize in the future.

Several lines of research provide some guidelines for how to be most helpful to a fearful person trying to learn a new approach. It has long been known that children and animals learn faster when they receive positive, supportive guidance in a new task, as opposed to when they are punished for making errors. Studies of exposure treatment for specific phobias indicate that therapists who merely *instruct* patients to do particular exposure tasks get poorer results than those who accompany the phobic person and demonstrate the requested behavior, providing a supportive role model. In a study of OCD patients, therapists who were respectful, understanding, encouraging, and challenging more often achieved positive outcomes than those who were permissive, tolerant, and less directly involved. What does this research suggest about how to be most helpful to people with OCD while they undergo exposure and ritual prevention treatment?

First, it seems apparent that family members and spouses will be more helpful if they give positive rather than negative feedback. Pleased reactions to small gains, such as less washing or checking, shorter time taken to get ready, fewer piles of saved newspapers in the living room, etc., will help encourage a patient to continue to struggle with exposure plans. Such positive comments are especially helpful when progress is apparent but slow, and the task seems arduous. By contrast, critical comments—noticing only what a person has *not* accomplished, especially in reaction to small setbacks or slow gains—are only likely to discourage, and possibly lead a patient to give up his or her struggle. Of course, few can act like saints, never reacting angrily to behaviors that are both unpleasant and inconvenient. But a concerted attempt to notice the positive can be very helpful.

Second, offering to support OCD sufferers as they confront feared situations and providing ideas or asking questions to stimulate thinking about how best to resist rituals may be very helpful. That does not mean telling the sufferer what to do. There is a fine line between encouraging the OCD symptoms and helping eradicate them. In their wish to be helpful, some family members have grown accustomed to taking over tasks that the sufferer could no longer manage without fear, and carrying out rituals such as washing, cleaning, checking, and even repeating actions at the sufferer's request. As noted in the chapters on treatment, this taking over of tasks for the OCD sufferer must be stopped as soon as possible in the treatment program. It is best replaced by encouragement that the sufferer do these fearful tasks him- or herself, initially with support and later alone. Family members' own rituals should be stopped, not with angry relief, but with the understanding that this will be difficult for the person with OCD, and is in his or her best interests. Spouses and family members must find the line between being appropriately challenging and being understanding when an exposure process is too difficult to manage at the moment and should be briefly delayed.

Other research has found that some family members believe their afflicted relative could actually control rituals if only he or she tried harder. OCD patients whose relatives believe this are more likely to relapse after exposure treatment, since this belief is associated with perceived criticism and anger in the relative. Close family members who are much inconvenienced by the symptoms naturally react with anger and blame, but expressing a lot of this does little to help the situation. We hope this book has convinced most readers of the degree to which people who develop OCD feel trapped by it, unable to exercise their normal logical thought processes to reduce their overwhelming obsessive anxiety. Instead, they resort to compulsions which they know to be absurd, but feel compelled to do to relieve the intense fear. Very few of those with OCD would voluntarily choose to have these symptoms. It is hard to imagine that if you were able to rid yourself of this affliction by a simple effort of will, you would not have done so long ago. Although it is especially difficult because most family members have not shared the same experience, it is important to empathize with the pain and frustration that this disorder brings. The energy it takes to react angrily to a sufferer's fear is better spent searching for methods to successfully reduce that fear.

Living Without Symptoms

Many people with OCD become increasingly non-functional as their symptoms occupy larger and larger portions of their time. When treatment is successful, it can leave a void in daily routine. To fill the space previously taken by obsessions and compulsions, new activities and in some cases new skills may be needed. Social plans and occupational activities (paid or volunteer employment) can be of great help in preventing a return to OCD symptoms. Old behaviors will willingly re-turn if free time is not filled with more appropriate—and ultimately more rewarding—activities. Some people may become overly concerned that new ventures will fail, and therefore hesitate to pursue avenues that would lead to more normal functioning. Professional help, such as rehabilitation programs, may be necessary to correct more seriously dis-rupted lifestyles. This stage of recovery can be difficult, but it helps to remember all the challenges you overcame to come this far.

Summary

Several personal and interpersonal difficulties can compli-cate the recovery process, both during and after treatment for OCD symptoms. Along with depression and anxiety, prob-lems with social anxiety and an obsessive-compulsive per-sonality style may interfere with progress. It is best to address these problems directly. Family and marital relationships may become strained or family members may become over-involved in OCD symptoms, unwittingly aiding and abet-ting the disorder. Suggestions for providing support include avoiding criticism and negative feedback while noticing gains in a positive way. Some angry reactions on the part of relatives are, of course, natural and reasonable, but excessive expression of hostility will probably impede progress and long-term gains. Once gains are made in successfully reducing time spent on obsessions and compulsions, it's important to fill the extra time with meaningful and engaging activities.

13

Looking Toward the Future

This last chapter will discuss a variety of clinical and research issues that seem likely to affect future understanding and treatment of Obsessive Compulsive Disorder (OCD). These are the topics arousing researchers' interest and curiosity today, offering possible pathways to tomorrow's answers. Included among these topics are disorders that appear to be similar to OCD; personal characteristics that might contribute to the development of OCD, and subsequently affect the patient's ability to benefit from treatment; methods of preventing relapse following behavior therapy and drug treatment; and development of other types of treatment. Since the following pages look toward the future, some of the suggestions will be speculation. Only time will tell which of these ideas will be borne out—and which now unsuspected avenues will open up.

Issues in Diagnosis of OCD

There are many mental disorders with separate labels—trichotillomania (hair-pulling), nail-biting, kleptomania (compulsive stealing), hypochondriasis, body dysmorphic disorder (preoccupation that a part of one's body is deformed), exhibitionism, bulimia (binge-eating), anorexia, even Tourette's syndrome (a disorder of tics)—whose symptoms bear strong resemblances to OCD. Some (such as Tourette's syndrome) seem to show related familial patterns: the relative of a Tourette's patient has an increased risk of developing OCD, and vice versa, suggesting the disorders are related. Others (such as bulimia) show surprisingly high rates of co-occurrence with OCD: a third or more of all bulimics also exhibit some degree of OCD. Other disorders (such as trichotillomania or body dysmorphic disorder) seem to respond to treatments that are helpful for OCD. Sometimes one of these disorders (for example, anorexia) will later evolve into OCD, or vice versa.

All of these findings suggest that there may be a group of "obsessive compulsive disorders" much larger than typical OCD as it is currently defined. This could mean that the fundamental problem underlying OCD, whatever it is, may be much more widespread than is now suspected—even considering the new appreciation for the high prevalence (2 percent of the general population) of typical OCD. These findings also point to possibilities that treatments effective for OCD—serotonergic drugs and exposure with response prevention—may help people with these other problems as well.

Characteristics Associated With OCD

Several researchers and clinicians have observed that there appear to be particular mental traits characteristic of people with OCD. As you will see, several of these characteristics are interrelated.

One common trait was identified as "risk aversion" by Dr. Steven Rasmussen, a co-author of the Obsessive-Compulsive Symptoms Checklist, (see Appendix B), because so many OCD patients try to avoid any type of risk-taking. Although this is not true of all people with OCD, many live their lives struggling to minimize uncertainty, even when it proves quite inconvenient to do so. It is as if they would like to have control over everything, or at least most things, that happen in their lives. Of course many life-shaping events cannot be controlled because they happen randomly or because the power and control lie in the hands of other people. Some people have a harder time than others accepting this.

For example, one engineer disliked traveling too far from home. This was not so much because his checking compulsions made it difficult to leave the house, but because he felt going out was more risky than staying at home. In his own house, he felt he had some control over unfortunate events. His worries were rarely precisely defined, but usually concerned the house or his work or some misfortune that might occur on a trip—misfortune that would not have happened had he stayed home.

This man held a firm belief that risks should be avoided whenever possible. Clearly, his attitude led to a very restrictive lifestyle. It had become difficult to relax and have fun, since many forms of "fun" involve a bit of risk. Risk aversion is probably learned, either from an overly restrictive family upbringing or from personal experiences in which risk taking is followed by unpleasant consequences. However it is acquired, risk avoidance attitudes may render people more susceptible to developing OCD. The trait, if left unexamined, may also make it more difficult to overcome the disorder over the long term.

Another problem area appears to be *excessive guilt*. Many people with OCD experience strong feelings of guilt despite the absence of evidence suggesting that they are responsible for any unfortunate event. Sometimes guilt appears in the context of religious beliefs, especially Catholic, Jewish, or fundamentalist Christian religions. But often it seems to be independent of formal religious teachings. Usually the guilt-ridden person with OCD will recall having felt this way since childhood, and many remember following their parents teachings or example.

Several of our patients have recalled teachings from Catholic school that they felt were instrumental in their development of obsessive ideas. For example, one woman remembered being taught by nuns in second grade that "bad thoughts" (for example, being angry and wanting to hurt someone, having sexual fantasies) were sinful and would be punished by God. She further believed that God expected her to go to *any* extreme to rid herself of these thoughts. She remembered developing an idea of God as "out to get me." Her mother's somewhat rigid household rules and critical style supplemented her fears and provided a second source of guilt whenever she failed to meet expected standards. After much questioning by her therapist and exploration of why she believed this, as well as several conversations with a priest, she gradually let go of these unreasonable beliefs.

Another young woman whose OCD symptoms centered around contamination from animal feces and garbage became unable to practice her profession as a physical therapist. Her work impairment was not due to her fears of contamination, but rather to a concern that if her patients failed to improve, it would be her fault. She ascribed problematic treatments to her own errors in judgment, taking more responsibility than the situation warranted. You may recall the description in the first chapter of a woman unable to pick up money lying in the street because it did not belong to her. Her actions—or inactions—also betrayed an excessive tendency to feel guilty. Like risk aversion, excessive guilt seems to render people more susceptible to OCD symptoms and make recovery more problematic.

A third potential problem area may be *extreme perfectionism*: attitudes about the importance of doing things perfectly or correctly. This doesn't just mean a ritualistic ordering of objects or repetition of actions to "get it right" (although that may be included), but also the general belief that it is important to do things correctly. A related tendency toward *indecision*, for fear of making a mistake, seems to be another common trait of many OCD sufferers. It is as if some sufferers believe that being wrong or making an error is fundamentally bad and must be avoided at all costs. Again, such efforts seem to be rooted in early experience. The tendency might be reinforced by high parental standards for performance in school or in other activities, accompanied by criticism for failing to meet these standards.

One woman with OCD remembered clearly her father's words and exasperated tone, "If you're going to do it, do it right or don't do it at all!" Her conclusion was that mistakes were unacceptable. Not surprisingly, she hesitated frequently when faced with decisions as to whether or not she should try something new or consider a task complete.

It is important to note that sufferers' parents have not always encouraged such attitudes and behaviors. In fact, some parents sought to help their perfectionistic child relax his or her own standards, and learn to be more flexible and accepting of flaws. Some people with OCD appear to have high levels of internal discomfort (whether biologically or environmentally determined) that propel them to seek control over a disorderly world. In fact, most of the above discussed traits (risk aversion, guilt perfectionism, and indecision) seem to be efforts to control events that are at least somewhat unpredictable by their very nature, and therefore uncontrollable.

To overcome OCD symptoms that seem to be rooted in these traits, and to inoculate people against a return of OCD symptoms in the future, it may be necessary to alter such core beliefs. Fundamental drives to avoid taking risks or accepting less-than-perfect performance, as well as strong feelings of excessive responsibility and guilt, probably need to be addressed directly. One therapist of Dr. White's acquaintance encouraged patients to aspire to become "Alexander the Adequate" rather than "Alexander the Great!"

To accomplish this, new methods of cognitive therapy for OCD may have to be developed. Current cognitive techniques have proven quite effective in alleviating depression when they have focused on helping depressed people modify distorted thinking processes and erroneous assumptions. But this type of cognitive therapy has so far not been very useful for OCD. The problem may be that the treatments tested have not focused on the types of core beliefs discussed above. If research can show that these traits are indeed characteristic of many people with OCD, then the next few years should see the development of effective cognitive treatments directed specifically at such erroneous thinking patterns. Perhaps this will inhibit the development of OCD in some cases, and offer hope for more complete and lasting recovery in others.

Cognitive Compulsions and Coping Skills

As discussed in earlier chapters, it is important to identify mental compulsions as such, since these mental processes serve the same function as behavioral rituals. That is, mental rituals *reduce* discomfort—as opposed to obsessions, which *cause* the discomfort. Rituals prevent OCD sufferers from learning that if they wait out the discomfort without ritualizing, the obsessive fear will decrease on its own. We believe that the frequency of mental rituals is probably much higher than previously thought, because mental health clinicians simply did not ask people with OCD detailed questions about their thinking processes. Initial investigation supports the idea that some thoughts increase anxiety (obsessions), and are soon followed by other thoughts that decrease it (mental compulsions). The relieving thoughts may last only for a brief period, at which point the obsessions intrude again. Indeed, the period of anxiety relief may be so brief that the person is almost unaware of it, until he or she is asked to describe the immediately preceding thoughts.

This is a confusing issue. It can be difficult to decide whether an OCD sufferer's mental efforts to calm him- or herself are really mental rituals, or whether they are helpful coping strategies. Do you feel *compelled* to think these thoughts, or are they another form of deliberate logical argument or self-talk that actually helps to whittle away at your unreasonable obsessive ideas? This distinction can be very difficult—and important—to make.

If mental rituals are indeed common, and prove to delay the process of recovery through exposure treatment, then it will be important to develop treatments that help block the mental rituals. One such treatment has been suggested by Dr. Paul Salkovis, who used tape-recorded playback of obsessive thoughts with the deliberate omission of mental rituals. Listening to taped obsessions exposes patients to their feared ideas while preventing them from running through their mental compulsions. This method sounds promising, but it has only been tried in a few cases. More information is needed about the frequency of mental rituals, and about the effectiveness of tape-recorded exposure, before OCD patients can be advised with certainty how best to deal with this problem.

New Drugs for Treatment of OCD

The current trend in research is to search for drugs with ever more specific effects on serotonin, the neurotransmitter thought central to OCD. (Chapters 3 and 10 provide more detailed discussions of serotonin theory and OCD drug therapy.) Meanwhile, serotonin uptake inhibitors remain the mainstay of drug therapy for OCD, but the search is on for such drugs with fewer side effects. Fluvoxamine, for example, probably has fewer side effects than clomipramine, and may even have fewer than Prozac; sertraline is another serotonin uptake inhibitor with a low profile of side effects being studied for OCD.

Efforts are also underway to enhance the effects of these serotonin uptake inhibitors with the addition of other drugs —for example, lithium, fenfluramine (Pondimin), or trazedone (Desyrel). It may be that such drug combinations can result in greater symptom reduction than any single drug.

OCD sufferers are often by nature reluctant to try new, "experimental" drugs. Keep in mind, however, that this is the way standard treatments are improved, and promising new treatments introduced. Generally, new drugs are studied because they are thought to have potential advantages over older drugs. Placebo controls are necessary because they rule out effects of suggestion and time, and they also offer OCD sufferers a monitored chance to see what they can do "on their own."

As researchers, we have tried throughout this book to encourage people to look favorably on the opportunity to participate in research whenever available. Personal benefit is of course a primary goal. But it can be enhanced by the knowledge that you are helping others by contributing to a better understanding of OCD and a gradual improvement in treatment options.

Preventing Relapse When Drugs Are Withdrawn

This issue remains problematic. Lifelong treatment with medication is something few people like to contemplate. But OCD is typically a chronic illness, and therapeutic effects of drugs usually fade away within weeks or months of their discontinuation. Behavior therapy seems to offer the main hope of successfully stopping drugs without severe relapse. Another avenue is simply to accept the need for indefinite medication, just as a diabetic must accept the need for lifelong insulin. Unpleasant as this prospect may seem, at least you can be reassured that some of these drugs have seen three decades of use, without any long-term serious ill effects.

Family Therapy for OCD

So far, there has been almost no research on the effects of family therapy for families in which one member suffers from OCD. Family therapy is now widely practiced by many mental health professionals. Some even identify themselves as "family therapists," and treat individuals only in the context of their family situation. In view of the often far-reaching effects of OCD on other family members, it seems important to determine whether OCD sufferers and those closest to them might benefit substantially from joint treatment.

An advantage of seeing the family as a whole is that everyone exposed to the OCD symptoms is given an opportunity to voice reactions and learn more about the disorder. Some centers for the treatment of OCD (including Dr. Steven Rasmussen's at Butler Hospital in Providence, RI, and our own clinic in Boston) have instituted family psychoeducational group programs. These allow families of OCD members to meet together on an ongoing basis, with a professional staff member, to learn more about the disorder and how to manage situations in the home.

Families of OCD sufferers often find themselves particularly caught up in the disorder, both in its perpetuation and in its treatment. One area, in particular, in which difficulties may arise during exposure and ritual prevention treatment is that of reassurance for the person with OCD. People with OCD often seek reassurance that a situation is safe or has been checked properly, behavior that in itself can become ritualistic. It is important that family members who become part of such a ritual know how to respond to such questions. Since exposure to feared obsessive ideas is critical for improvement, repeated requests for reassurance must be met with polite refusal. It should be clear that the relative does not mean to be unkind, but does not want to foster dependence on reassurance from others. The goal is to encourage the OCD sufferer's trust in his or her own knowledge of the facts. Maintaining such behavior, let alone understanding the need for it, can be a great challenge to concerned families.

Similarly, family members often become embroiled in carrying out rituals or avoidance patterns because they have been asked to do so by their afflicted relative. It is not surprising that such restrictions on a family's behavior often lead to resentment. Apart from the irritation and frustration these demands engender, they are also unhelpful to the person with OCD: they allow continued avoidance and rituals, thereby preventing exposure. Of course, it is very difficult and often guilt-provoking to refuse these requests, particularly when the OCD sufferer has not yet decided to embark on a behavioral treatment program.

To address these problems, as well as many others that arise in families with a member who has OCD, a treatment program that includes all family members can undoubtedly be helpful. Such a program might include spouses or families in occasional sessions in an otherwise individual treatment program for the person with OCD; or it might focus on treating the entire family as a group. Another option is to form a psychoeducational family group to provide information and foster discussion among multiple families with this problem. One clear lesson from the research literature is that for married people with OCD, traditional marital therapy is not an effective treatment. Marital therapy may improve the marriage, but it has relatively little effect, as you might expect, on OCD symptoms. Exposure treatment, on the other hand, tends to improve both the OCD symptoms and marital happiness.

Here again, not enough information is yet known to determine the best way to involve family members in treatment. No doubt the future will see continued experimentation in this area, leading to more comprehensive treatment programs that are maximally helpful to OCD sufferers and their family members.

Support Groups

Recently, the surge of awareness of and interest in OCD has led to the founding of OCD support groups. These are groups of people with the disorder (and sometimes family members or friends) who meet regularly to discuss and find solutions to their problems. Some groups have adopted a particular focus, such as a 12-step program adapted for OCD; other groups set their own educational and self-help agenda. Such groups offer sufferers the opportunity to feel connected to others who share similar burdens. They can be a powerful experience for many who have felt isolated and ashamed of their problems. Although no research has yet been done on such groups, we believe they may be helpful in motivating sufferers to seek effective treatments, in confronting and coping with fears and compulsions more effectively, and in preventing relapse after successful behavior therapy. It seems doubtful that support groups can replace individual behavioral and drug therapies (administered by experienced practitioners) as a treatment for OCD; but they can undoubtedly augment the benefits of these treatments. To locate a group in your area, contact the OCD Foundation in New Haven, CT.

Summary and Comments

The above discussion has highlighted some of the areas likely to receive further research and clinical attention in the future. They hold promise for people with OCD and their families, the more so as each research study contributes to knowledge.

Throughout this book we have tried to provide information about OCD and its treatment, with an eye toward giving sufferers some of the tools necessary to control their symptoms. It remains true that, with treatment strategies currently available, a "cure" is probably not a reasonable goal. Rather, very substantial improvement can be achieved via exposure to feared obsessive situations and severe restriction of ritualistic thoughts and actions. Medication treatment can also lead to significant improvement. As people gain confidence in their ability to tolerate exposure to uncomfortable situations and resist carrying out rituals, they are increasingly able to apply this knowledge in future situations when obsessive anxiety becomes a problem. Medications may assist in helping people gain control over ritualistic impulses and thus prevent further development of unreasonable fears.

Family members can assist in this process by encouraging exposure, and by refraining from criticism, from helping OCD sufferers avoid uncomfortable situations, or from participating in ritualistic acts for the patient's sake. As also noted, some traits seem to increase chances that a person will develop OCD, and also that the recovered OCD sufferer will return to obsessive and compulsive symptoms in the future. These traits include perfectionism, avoidance of risk, a tendency to feel guilty easily, and a fear of making mistakes. Although no one yet knows how best to address these problems, we believe they may require some attention to prevent future development of OCD in former sufferers. Family members who believe they share some of these traits might also wish to work on modifying them, since these characteristics do not appear to be helpful models for OCD sufferers.

We realize that many who read this book may need the assistance of a professional mental health person—a psychiatrist, psychologist, social worker, or psychiatric nurse—to overcome their OCD symptoms. If you are in doubt as to whether you can carry out the program presented here yourself, try it first. But if you encounter difficulty, find yourself looking for ways to make it easier, or sense that you are avoiding exposure, do not hesitate to seek out a therapist skilled in treatment of OCD as a consultant in the treatment process. This book is intended both as a self-help method, and as a bibliographic aid during treatment with a professional. Thousands have recovered normal functioning with appropriate treatment; we encourage you to muster your courage and try the procedures suggested here. It is indeed difficult, but you have little to lose by doing so and so much to gain.

Appendix A

Annotated Bibliography on Obsessive Compulsive Disorder

Emmelkamp, P.M.G. (1982). *Phobic and Obsessive-Compulsive Disorders: Theory, Research and Practice. New York: Plenum Press.* This volume presents research on OCD conducted by Emmelkamp and his colleagues in Holland, as well as by other researchers. Five chapters focus specifically on OCD.

Foa, E.B. and Kozak, M.J. (1986). Emotional processing of fear: Exposure to corrective information. *Psychological Bulletin, 99,* 20-35. This article presents a theoretical view of anxiety disorders, among them obsessive-compulsive disorder, and proposes treatment methods which would be expected to be helpful. This is difficult reading intended for a professional audience.

Insel, T.R. (Ed.) (1984). *New Findings in Obsessive-Compulsive Disorders.* Washington, D.C.: American Psychiatric Press. This 120-page monograph has 6 chapters by experts in the field, covering the clinical picture, childhood OCD, and psychodynamic, behavioral, pharmacological, and cognitive treatments for OCD.

Marks, I.M. (1987). *Fears, Phobias and Rituals.* New York: Oxford University Press. This book covers anxiety disorders in general, with specific OCD chapters on classification, clinical aspects, and behavioral and pharmacological treatments.

Mavissakalian, M., Turner, S.M., and Michelson, L. (Eds.) (1985). *Obsessive-Compulsive Disorders: Psychological and Pharmacological Treatment.* New York: Plenum Press. This edited volume includes chapters by leading experts on clinical issues, research on behavioral therapy, psychodynamic psychotherapy, pharmacotherapy, and future directions.

Meyer, V., (1966). Modification of expectations in cases with obsessional rituals, *Behavior Research and Therapy, 4,* 273-280. This article represents the first application of exposure and ritual prevention treatment.

Meyer, V., Levy, R., and Schnurer, A. (1974). A behavioral treatment of obsessive-compulsive disorders. In H.R. Beech (Ed.), *Obsessional States,* London: Methuen. This chapter elaborates on Dr. Meyer's exposure and ritual prevention treatment and presents results for 15 cases.

Rachman, S.J., and Hodgson, R. (1980). *Obsessions and Compulsions.* New York: Prentice-Hall. This book covers all aspects of OCD from clinical features and course of illness to behavioral treatments developed and researched by these authors over many years. Research on drug treatment is not up to date, since the book was published a decade ago.

Rasmussen, S.A. and Eisen, J.L. (1989). Clinical features and phenomenology of obsessive-compulsive disorder, *Psychiatric Annals*, 19, 67-73. This article reviews previous research on types of symptoms, diagnostic issues, and developmental precursors of OCD.

Reed, G.F. (1985). *Obsessional Experience and Compulsive* Behavior. Orlando, Fl.: Academic Press. This volume covers both OCD and OC personality disorder, with respect to natural history, theoretical issues, and cognitive characteristics and behavioral and cognitive treatments.

Salkovskis, P.M. and Westbrook, D. (1989). Behaviour therapy and obsessional ruminations: can failure be turned into success? *Behaviour Research and Therapy*, 17, 149-160. This article discusses the confusion of obsessions with mental rituals and the need to treat each differently.

Salzman, L. (1979). Psychotherapy of the obsessional, *American Journal of Psychotherapy*, 33, 32-40. This article presents a psychodynamic treatment method for obsessive-compulsive symptoms.

See also Dr. Salzna's chapter. "Comments on the Psychological Treatment of Obsessive Compulsive Patients" in the edited book by Mavissakalian, Turner and Michelson cited earlier.

Sifneos. P.E. (1985). Short-term dynamic psychotherapy for patients suffering from an obsessive-compulsive disorder. In the edited book by Mavissakalian, Turner and Michelson cited earlier. This chapter explains Dr. Sifneos psychodynamic treatment method for OCD.

Steketee, G., and Foa, E.B. (1985). "Obsessive-Compulsive Disorder." In D.H. Barlow (Ed.), *Clinical Handbook of Psychological Disorders*. New York: Guilford Press. pp. 69-144. This lengthy chapter provides detailed instructions for mental health practitioners on how to treat OCD from a behavioral perspective, including common problems during and after treatment.

Turner, S.M., and Beidel, D.C. (1988). *Treating Obsessive Compulsive Disorder*. Elmsford, N.Y.: Pergamon Press. This is a 110-page monograph covering diagnosis and behavioral and biological treatments for OCD.

Relaxation Tapes

Bernstein, D.A., and Borkovec, T.D. (1973). *Progressive Relaxation Training*. Champaign, Il.: Research Press. (Record included.)

Cotler, S.B., and Guerra, J.J. *Self-Relaxation Training* (audiocassette). Champaign, Il.: Research Press.

Appendix B

Obsessive-Compulsive Symptoms Checklist

(Modified from a checklist developed by Goodman, W.K., Price, L.H., Mazure, C., Heninger, G.R., and Charney, D.S., Department of Psychiatry, Yale University School of Medicine and by Rasmussen, S.A., Department of Psychiatry, Brown University School of Medicine.)

Check all that apply, and clearly mark the principal symptoms with a "p."

Aggressive Obsessions

- ☐ Fear of harming yourself
- ☐ Fear of harming others
- ☐ Trouble with violent or horrific images
- ☐ Fear of blurting out obscenities or insults
- ☐ Fear of doing something else embarrassing
- ☐ Fear that you will act on unwanted impulses (e.g., to stab a loved one)
- ☐ Fear that you will harm others by not being careful enough (e.g., driving over someone)
- ☐ Fear that you will be responsible for something else terrible happening (e.g., fire, burglary)

Contamination Obsessions

- ☐ Concern or disgust with bodily waste or secretions (e.g., urine, feces, saliva)
- ☐ Concern with dirt or germs
- ☐ Excessive concern with environmental contaminants (e.g., asbestos, radiation, toxic waste)
- ☐ Excessive concern with household chemicals or cleansing agents
- ☐ Excessive concern with animals (e.g., insects)
- ☐ Fear of sticky substances or residues
- ☐ Concern that you will get ill
- ☐ Concern that you will get others ill
- ☐ Concern with diseases (e.g., AIDS, hepatitis, VD)

Trouble With Sexual Obsessions

- ☐ Forbidden or perverse sexual thoughts, images, or impulses
- ☐ Thoughts or impulses involving children or incest
- ☐ Thoughts or impulses involving homosexuality
- ☐ Inappropriate sexual behavior toward others

Trouble With Hoarding/Saving Obsessions

- ☐ Examples: magazines, papers, trash, objects

Religious Obsessions (scrupulosity)

- ☐ Concern with sacrilege and blasphemy, sinfulness
- ☐ Excessive concern with right and wrong, morality
- ☐ Trouble with religious images or thoughts

Obsession With Need for Symmetry, Exactness, or Order

Somatic Obsessions

- ☐ Concern with illness or disease
- ☐ Excessive concern with body parts or aspect of appearance

Cleaning/Washing Compulsions

- ☐ Excessive handwashing
- ☐ Excessive showering or bathing
- ☐ Excessive toothbrushing, grooming, or toilet routine
- ☐ Excessive cleaning of household items or other objects
- ☐ Use of special cleansers to remove "contamination"
- ☐ Use of other measures to prevent contact with or remove "contamination"

Checking Compulsions

- ☐ Need to check that you did not/will not harm others
- ☐ Need to check that you did not/will not harm self
- ☐ Need to check that nothing terrible did/will happen
- ☐ Need to check that you did not make a mistake
- ☐ Need to check because of somatic obsessions (e.g., checking body parts)

Repeating Rituals

- ☐ Need to re-read or re-write

☐ Need to repeat routine activities (e.g., crossing thresholds, going in/out door, up/down from chair, tying shoes, dressing/undressing

Counting Compulsions

Ordering/Arranging Compulsions

Hoarding/Collecting Compulsions

Miscellaneous Obsessions

☐ Need to know or remember
☐ Fear of saying certain things
☐ Fear of not saying just the right thing
☐ Fear of losing things
☐ Trouble with intrusive (neutral) images
☐ Trouble with intrusive nonsense sounds, words, or music
☐ Bothered by certain sounds/noises
☐ Fear of making mistakes
☐ Concern with certain colors
☐ Superstitious fears
☐ Concern with certain numbers

Miscellaneous Compulsions

☐ Mental rituals (other than checking or counting)
☐ Need to tell or confess
☐ Need to touch, tap, or rub
☐ Measures to prevent (not by checking): harm to self; harm to others; terrible consequences

- ☐ Ritualized eating behaviors
- ☐ Superstitious actions
- ☐ Pulling hairs (from scalp, eyebrows, eyelashes, pubic hair)
- ☐ Acts of self-damage or self-mutilation (such as picking face)
- ☐ Request for reassurance from others

Other New Harbinger Self-Help Titles

The Relaxation & Stress Reduction Workbook, 3rd Edition, $13.95
Leader's Guide to the Relaxation & Stress Reduction Workbook, $14.95
Beyond Grief: A Guide for Recovering from the Death of a Loved One,
    $10.95
Thoughts & Feelings: The Art of Cognitive Stress Intervention, $12.95
Messages: The Communication Skills Book, $11.95
The Divorce Book, $10.95
Hypnosis for Change: A Manual of Proven Techniques, 2nd Edition,
    $11.95
The Deadly Diet: Recovering from Anorexia & Bulimia, $11.95
Self-Esteem, $11.95
The Better Way to Drink, $10.95
Chronic Pain Control Workbook, $12.50
Rekindling Desire, $10.95
Life Without Fear: Anxiety and Its Cure, $9.95
Visualization for Change, $11.95
Guideposts to Meaning, $10.95
Controlling Stagefright, $10.95
Videotape: Clinical Hypnosis for Stress & Anxiety Reduction, $24.95
*Starting Out Right: Essential Parenting Skills for Your Child's First
    Seven Years,* $12.95
Big Kids: A Parent's Guide to Weight Control for Children, $10.95
Personal Peace: Transcending Your Interpersonal Limits, $10.95
My Parent's Keeper: Adult Children of the Emotionally Disturbed, $11.95
When Anger Hurts, $11.95
Free of the Shadows: Recovering from Sexual Violence, $11.95
Resolving Conflict With Others and Within Yourself, $11.95
Liftime Weight Control, $10.95
When Once Is Not Enough, $11.95
Getting to Sleep, $10.95

Send a check or purchase order for the titles you
want, plus $2.00 for shipping and handling, to:

New Harbinger Publications
Department B
5674 Shattuck Avenue
Oakland, CA 94609

Or write for a free catalog of all our quality self-help
publications.